MW01516231

VEGETABLE GARDENING

Build step-by-step your garden simply and easily.

Grow Vegetables, Flowers, Fruits and Herbs at home even if you are a beginner.

Include a year-round growing plan.

RICHARD GREENWOOD

Table of Contents

Introduction

Vegetable gardening includes choosing a site, planning the garden, preparing the soil, selecting the plants and seeds, planting a crop, and cultivating the plants until they are ready for harvest. The final result is a new product to consume, share, or market.

Anyone willing to spend some time daily or 2 to nurture the crops may grow a vegetable garden. It does not take a good deal of cash, time, or ability, though some of each will be useful. With practice and patience, your skills will improve each year. Do not be discouraged if the first effort is not a massive success.

Growing veggies takes some distance, but not always acres. A vegetable garden may be on the floor or within a planting bed. However, it does not need to be. Many vegetables can be raised in containers. By way of instance, sufficient lettuce for a salad could be grown at a 12-inch kettle on the rear deck. Insert several radishes and carrots, also raised in 12-inch containers, like sweetness and spice, and you get a fantastic start on a yummy salad.

Success, however, takes more than only somewhere to grow the vegetables. They need sun, water, atmosphere, soil, fertilizer, and maintenance.

There are many benefits to incorporating more organic choices into your life, which is why more people around the world are choosing to go natural. At first, going organic may seem to be more expensive. And yes, many organic options in your local grocery store are indeed pricier. However, over time you can find that living a natural lifestyle can save you money! By choosing organic, you can benefit the health of your family, your home and yard, and even the planet. Many studies have found that by going natural people experience a wealth of physical benefits and a reduced risk of disease, saving you money on medical bills in the future.

One way you can begin your organic life is with growing your organic garden. By doing this, not only will you be provided with natural, fresh, local, in-season produce, but it will also be available at a fraction of the price.

When you practice organic gardening, you learn that the earth has many natural and organic options to feed into a cycle of sustainability. The ground is fully equipped to allow plants to flourish without the need for harmful chemicals or pesticides. If you use the knowledge of the earth, you can learn to start organic gardening literally from the ground up. You begin with the soil you are planting into the water and fertilizer that you feed the plants with. Over time, as you use these techniques, you will find that both your yard and your garden flourish, providing you with a wealth of ingredients that only have to travel from your backyard to your kitchen table.

By reading this book, you can learn to live a healthier and happier life through the power of organic gardening. Providing your body and mind with the foods, it craves you will soon find that you feel better than ever and have the satisfaction of knowing that you know exactly what you are eating.

Get ready to change your life!

Chapter 1: Types of Vegetable Gardening

Best Gardens for Beginners

What do you envision when you think of a vegetable garden? Vegetables in neat, uniform rows in a dedicated plot of land? But an in-ground garden isn't necessarily the best option for a beginner.

In-ground gardens can be highly productive, but there are variables you can't always control the first year, such as soil quality and pH. You also might have to clear the new land, perhaps tilling it or covering the soil for several months before planting.

Issues such as these are why container gardening and raised beds are so popular. Let's explore your options.

Container Gardening

In a container garden, vegetables and herbs grow in a limited space, such as a pot or large planter. Many beginners enjoy container gardens because the labor involved is minimal. You don't have to prepare the ground, and weeding is almost nonexistent. You can also place your pots in the best location for the plants you're growing.

But container gardening isn't free of challenges. The cost of the containers and soil can add up. Plants in containers require great attention to watering, and in the heat of summer may need watering several times per day. Container plants also need more fertilization, because the continual watering leaches away nutrients and the plants cannot access nutrients in the ground soil.

With proper attention and care, however, container gardens are rewarding. Great options for container growing include lettuce, greens, snap peas, peppers, tomatoes, and herbs.

Raised Bed Gardening

Raised beds combine the best features of in-ground and container gardens. Like containers, with proper mulching, you won't need to weed as often. But unlike containers, the plants' ability to send their roots into the native soil to access water and nutrients cuts down on both watering and fertilizing. Raised bed gardens, when done right, are very attractive. (Many people build raised beds on top of a solid surface such as paved ground. This design acts more like a container garden in terms of soil, water, fertilization, and drainage requirements.)

The biggest downside to raised beds is the initial cost and labor. You also cannot easily move them if you change your mind about the ideal location. Predesigned kits available at garden centers make the labor barrier easier to overcome.

Most gardeners who choose raised beds find the trade-offs to be worth it both in time saved over the season and their overall gardening experience. Almost all crops grow well in raised beds; some popular ones include tomatoes, beans, broccoli, peppers, onions, and zucchini.

Vertical Gardening

Whether you choose an in-ground garden, a container garden, a raised bed garden, or a combination of all three, consider adding vertical gardening to your plan. When you train vining plants on a trellis, you make space for more crops in the container or bed. Plus, the better airflow achieved with vertical gardening reduces the risk of many common plant diseases. Exercise your creative side: You can use free materials such as gathered sticks to build a trellis or make a small investment in a cattle-panel arch trellis. Sturdy trellises can last for many seasons. Great crops for vertical gardening include pole beans, climbing peas, cucumbers, and even melons.

Growing in the Ground

Maybe you don't have the budget for containers or raised beds. Or maybe you've always wanted a traditional in-ground garden, and you're determined to make it happen. Here are five qualities to look for when choosing to grow your garden directly in the ground.

Soil pH and balanced nutrients. The health of your garden soil will directly correspond to the health and productivity of your plants. I recommend getting your soil tested at a professional lab. Most counties offer this service through their cooperative extension locations for free or a small fee. From there, you will know what amendments you need to add to the soil if any.

Loamy soil mixture. Soil is made up of sand, silt, clay, or a combination of them. The ideal garden soil is loamy, meaning it has a balanced mixture of these components. If your soil leans heavily toward one element, your yields will not be as great. A professional soil test will tell you what soil type you have, and you can always amend a less-than-loamy soil with organic matter such as compost. But do note that it can take years to see a big difference.

Well-draining area. Plants will not thrive in standing water, so unless your soil contains a high amount of sand, you'll want to place your in-ground garden in an area that is slightly elevated or at least not lower than the surrounding land.

Slight slope. Ideal in-ground gardens have an almost undetectable slope. This means the land will drain well, but its gentle angle will also prevent nutritious topsoil and protective mulch from washing away during heavy rainfalls.

Away from trees. Trees inhibit growth in two ways. First, roots that extend under a garden steal water and nutrients. Second, trees shade the garden, which is not ideal for plants that need full sun.

Chapter 2: Planning Your Vegetable Gardening

Gardening is good therapy. There are many therapeutic aspects of gardening. The quietness of working among the flowers and vegetables is proven to slow our breathing and help us relax both mentally and physically. Quiet time in the garden also allows us to restructure our thoughts and work things out in our minds. It's hard to stay mad or feel like there's nothing right in your world when you are surrounded by the sight and smell of flowers and knowing that before long you'll be eating the things you've helped grow.

Gardening provides a sense of accomplishment. Does this even need an explanation? How can you not get a confidence boost when you see little seedlings popping up through the soil and then watch those seedlings get another set of leaves, then another, until they become everything there is supposed to be? Sitting down to eat a meal you've prepared with the tomatoes, green beans, lettuce, or whatever else you might have grown is priceless.

Gardening is a great way to get in shape and stay healthy. Bending, standing, hoeing, raking, pulling weeds, deadheading flowers, carrying a water can and dragging a hose around is exercise. No, you're not going to burn off enough calories to eat a giant piece of chocolate cake every day. Still, it's great cardio that will keep your heart rate up and burn more fat than you would by sitting around all day.

The vitamin D you derive from soaking up some sunshine is great for your health, too. There is a catch to this, though. Your chances of absorbing vitamin D from the sun are drastically reduced when you wear sunscreen with an SPF over 8. This leaves you wondering which is better—the vitamin D or protection from the sun. The answer is both. While you shouldn't prolong your exposure to the sun without some form of protection, the sun's rays are one of the few natural sources of vitamin D. Vitamin D is essential for strong, healthy bones, the formation of blood cells, and strengthening the immune system. It can also help absorb phosphorus and calcium and is often used to help people recover from or fight off certain diseases and illnesses, such as rickets, eczema, psoriasis and jaundice.

Gardening teaches responsibility. All kids need chores. All adults need chores, too—things that we are solely responsible for getting done. Things that if not done properly, will have negative outcomes. We need these chores so that we can learn to be responsible. So that we can witness first-hand what it means to see something to completion. So that we can feel accomplished and so that we can make a positive contribution to our existence. None of us should be content with just being here. We need to want to make our world a better place.

If you give children the responsibility of weeding, watering, and deadheading flowers—either in a flower garden or in pots—not only will they learn to be responsible, they will learn about the process of how things grow and what it takes to keep things growing at optimal levels. They will (or should) also learn what happens when they act responsibly... or not, i.e. earning an allowance, having flowers or vegetables to enjoy and sell, learning to use what they grow in different ways, etc.

We, adults, need to be reminded of the importance of responsibility, too. Often we get so wrapped up in what we want and what we think we need, that we become a bit selfish.

Gardening can save money. Most people I know don't regularly purchase fresh-cut flowers to enjoy. It's just one of those things we don't bother with. Unless that is, you are the type of person who is conscientious about supporting local growers by buying them from a farmer's market. But if you grow your own, you can save money and have flowers throughout your growing season.

How to Build Your Vegetable Gardening

People who have been gardening for a very long time use raised beds to avoid an array of challenges to gardening. Gardening in raised beds is so easy that a beginner can do it.

You can get rid of the bad dirt because you control the soil and compost blend you put into your raised bed garden. You build drainage into the walls, which still holds the soil and keeps erosion from happening. Raised beds get more sun exposure, which means that it gets warmer and allows for more diversity in the plants and longer growing season. You can place the plants closer together, therefore you yield more, weeds are crowded out, and water use is maximized. Also, raising the soil level even just twelve inches- one foot- greatly reduces the back-breaking effort of planting, weeding, and harvesting.

Raised bed gardens are a dream come true for a gardener. With all those positives, what is not to love about them? While building a raised bed garden isn't all that complicated, here are the steps you need to take to make your own raised bed garden.

1) Before you can get started, you must figure out how big you want your raised bed to be. If you're not sure how big you want it to be, then you should first start with a four by four-foot square, which is the distance that most people can reach the middle from either side. Then, you will want to level the ground so that your raised bed will be completely flat.

A raised bed that is three by six will be wide enough to support tomatoes, but yet still narrow enough that you can reach it from both sides. Ideally, you want to make it one to two feet tall. You can make it taller, but keep in mind that the bigger you make it, the more soil you will need.

Make sure that you find a fairly flat spot. It will save you a lot of time and effort in the preparation process. After all, you want your walls to be level, right? As far as placement, the general rule is that a North-South placement can take advantage of the available light all day long. Try to avoid areas that are shaded by the house or by trees. Also, if building multiple beds, you will want to leave at least eighteen inches between so that you can walk through, or if you will need room for a lawnmower or wheelbarrow, leave two feet.

2) Make your walls. To start, get 4 one-foot long four by fours to create the corner posts, 8 four-foot long two by sixes for the side rails, and 4 two-foot long two by twos for the center stakes.

Put your four by fours on each corner of the area you marked off. Starting with all of your choices, screw in your first two by six to secure the corners together. Stack another two by six on top of the first. Make sure that your ends are even with the ends of the posts. You can use an angle-square to be sure that the rails and posts are lined up correctly.

You will want to build the walls separately then fasten them together before putting the raised bed into position. Placing the corner posts and posts halfway along the walls offers stability for your raised bed, so you want to do this. They will also help to hold your bed in place and reduce the pressure that the soil will exert on your frame. You can use a cap railing around the top of the frame to tie it all together and offer you a great place to lay down your tools while you are working, or sit and admire your handiwork. You can get bed covers to keep insects away and keep your plants warm in the cooler weather.

These instructions use wood to create raised beds. You can use bricks if you wish, or you can use wood to create frames and then use sheet metal for the walls. You should remember that if you are using lumber, you need to use wood that has not been persevered with toxins. Make sure to stay away from creosote railroad ties- instead, choose cedar or redwood, which is naturally rot-resistant. Another option is ACQ (alkaline copper quaternary) treated wood, and it is safe for food crops. However, you might want to consider using landscape fabric between it and the soil to keep them from coming in contact. Use galvanized or stainless screws or bolts to put them together, regardless of the type of wood you use.

3) Connect the walls. You will now stand the sidewalls up and opposite of each other with the corner posts on the outside.

4) Now, you want to square it up. To do this, you will measure diagonally in both directions across the planter to make sure the frame is exactly square. Adjust your raised bed until both of the diagonals are equal lengths.

5) Make your walls sturdy. Take the two by two stakes and place in the middle of each of the outside walls, and pound it into the ground so that the top of the stake is level with the top of the wall.

6) Fill your raised bed with topsoil. Once your bed is complete, it is time to fill it. You will want to use quality topsoil, especially if your natural ground isn't conducive to plant growth. You may also want to add organic materials such as peat moss or compost after you have done all this and watered the soil well, its time to start planting your plants.

Make sure that you don't get soil from the ground- especially if your natural ground isn't conducive to growing plants. Use compost, a soil mix, or even peat moss for your raised beds. You will want to use a two by four to level out the soil and then you can plant. If space allows, consider building more than one bed, which will make life much easier- you can rotate crops and make sure that you can meet the watering needs of each individual type of plant. If you line up the beds in rows, you simplify the process of installing an irrigation system.

7) You can create a framework for a lightweight cover with hoops and extend the growing season in the cooler areas, conserve moisture in the drier areas, and protect plants from insects or birds. To do this, you will use galvanized pipes to mount one-inch PVC pipes inside of the raised bed walls. Then, cut ½-inch flexible PVC tube that is twice the width of the bed, bend it, mount it, and

attach it. You should use a clear film to raise the air and soil temperatures in the early fall or spring to help you get an early start on planting. Be careful that you don't bake your plants on the warmer days. To avoid excess heat buildup, you will want to either remove the cover or cut slits in it. To control pests, cover the bed with row covers, which are a gauzelike fabric, or bird netting. These will let in the air and the light, but keep out the flying insects.

As was mentioned before, you can find pre-made, boxed raised garden beds, so you don't have to go to the hassle of making your own. If you do want to make your own, you can make it as large or as small as you like.

Chapter 3: How to Build Your Vegetable Gardening

People who have been gardening for a very long time use raised beds to avoid an array of challenges to gardening. Gardening in raised beds is so easy that a beginner can do it.

You can get rid of the bad dirt because you control the soil and compost blend you put into your raised bed garden. You build drainage into the walls, which still holds the soil and keeps erosion from happening. Raised beds get more sun exposure, which means that it gets warmer and allows for more diversity in the plants and longer growing season. You can place the plants closer together; therefore, you yield more, weeds are crowded out, and water use is maximized. Also, raising the soil level even just twelve inches- one foot- greatly reduces the back-breaking effort of planting, weeding, and harvesting.

Raised bed gardens are a dream come true for a gardener. With all those positives, what is not to love about them? While building a raised bed garden isn't all that complicated, here are the steps you need to take to make your own raised bed garden.

1) Before you can get started, you must figure out how big you want your raised bed to be. If you're not sure how big you want it to be, then you should first start with a four by four-foot square, which is the distance that most people can reach the middle from either side. Then, you will want to level the ground so that your raised bed will be completely flat.

A raised bed that is three by six will be wide enough to support tomatoes, but yet still narrow enough that you can reach it from both sides. Ideally, you want to make it one to two feet tall. You can make it taller, but keep in mind that the bigger you make it, the more soil you will need.

Make sure that you find a fairly flat spot. It will save you a lot of time and effort in the preparation process. After all, you want your walls to be level, right? As far as placement, the general rule is that a North-South placement can take advantage of the available light all day long. Try to avoid areas that are shaded by the house or by trees. Also, if building multiple beds, you will want to leave at least eighteen inches between so that you can walk through, or if you will need room for a lawnmower or wheelbarrow, leave two feet.

2) Make your walls. To start, get 4 one-foot long four by fours to create the corner posts, 8 four-foot-long two by sixes for the side rails, and 4 two-foot-long two by twos for the center stakes.

Put your four by fours on each corner of the area you marked off. Starting with all of your choices, screw in your first two by six to secure the corners together. Stack another two by six on top of the first. Make sure that your ends are even with the ends of the posts. You can use an angle-square to be sure that the rails and posts are lined up correctly.

You will want to build the walls separately then fasten them together before putting the raised bed into position. Placing the corner posts and posts halfway along the walls offers stability for your raised bed, so you want to do this. They will also help to hold your bed in place and reduce the pressure that the soil will exert on your frame. You can use a cap railing around the top of the frame to tie it all together and offer you a great place to lay down your tools while you are working, or sit and admire your handiwork. You can get bed covers to keep insects away and keep your plants warm in the cooler weather.

These instructions use wood to create raised beds. You can use bricks if you wish, or you can use wood to create frames and then use sheet metal for the walls. There will be more on that later on. You should remember that if you are using lumber, you need to use wood that has not been persevered with toxins. Make sure to stay away from creosote railroad ties- instead, choose cedar or redwood, which is naturally rot-resistant. Another option is ACQ (alkaline copper quaternary) treated wood, and it is safe for food crops. However, you might want to consider using landscape fabric between it and the soil to keep them from coming in contact. Use galvanized or stainless screws or bolts to put them together, regardless of the type of wood you use.

3) Connect the walls together. You will now stand the sidewalls up and opposite of each other with the corner posts on the outside.

4) Now, you want to square it up. To do this, you will measure diagonally in both directions across the planter to make sure the frame is exactly square. Adjust your raised bed until both of the diagonals are equal lengths.

5) Make your walls sturdy. Take the two by two stakes and place in the middle of each of the outside walls, and pound it into the ground so that the top of the stake is level with the top of the wall.

6) Fill your raised bed with topsoil. Once your bed is complete, it is time to fill it. You will want to use quality topsoil, especially if your natural ground isn't conducive to plant growth. You may also want to add organic materials such as peat moss or compost.

After you have done all this and watered the soil well, its time to start planting your plants.

Make sure that you don't get soil from the ground- especially if your natural ground isn't conducive to growing plants. Use compost, a soil mix, or even peat moss for your raised beds. You will want to use a two by four to level out the soil and then you can plant. If space allows, consider building more than one bed, which will make life much easier- you can rotate crops and make sure that you can meet the watering needs of each individual type of plant. If you line up the beds in rows, you simplify the process of installing an irrigation system.

7) You can create a framework for a lightweight cover with hoops and extend the growing season in the cooler areas, conserve moisture in the drier areas, and protect plants from insects or birds. To do this, you will use galvanized pipes to mount one-inch PVC pipes inside of the raised bed walls. Then, cut ½-inch flexible PVC tube that is twice the width of the bed, bend it, mount it, and attach it. You should use a clear film to raise the air and soil temperatures in the early fall or spring to help you get an early start on planting. Be careful that you don't bake your plants on the warmer days. To avoid excess heat buildup, you will want to either remove the cover or cut slits in it. To control pests, cover the bed with row covers, which are a gauzelike fabric, or bird

netting. These will let in the air and the light, but keep out the flying insects.

As was mentioned before, you can find pre-made, boxed raised garden beds, so you don't have to go to the hassle of making your own. If you do want to make your own, you can make it as large or as small as you like. You can make it square, rectangle, hexagonal, basically any shape you can think of- as long as it has straight sides (it would be a little difficult to make a round one, but you could try).

Chapter 4: How to Plant Your Vegetable Gardening

Inter Planting

Also known as inter-cropping, this is a great planting strategy that gives you multiple crops from one raised bed. This is a great way to maximize your production and to use your raised beds efficiently.

This involves planting short-season vegetables in between long-season vegetables. You may plant out your tomatoes, which take a long time to mature and in between them plant vegetables that mature faster, such as spinach, lettuce, radishes, and so on. These vegetables are harvested and finished before the main crop plant has matured and crowded them out.

The main crop plants are planted out at their normal spacing as are the short season vegetables, but in between the main crop. Many people will plant lettuce and spinach in between their peppers, tomatoes, and eggplants as the main crop plants concentrate on establishing a root system at the start of the season whilst the short season plants use the top six inches or so of soil. A great tip is to sow radishes with your carrots or parsnips as the radishes grow very quickly and will mark where the row of the slower germinating carrots is.

The short season plants grow quickly and shade out weeds, helping the soil to retain moisture and acting as a barrier or deterrent to many pests who then struggle to find the main crop plants.

Another popular crop for interplanting is sweetcorn, with some people planting pumpkin plants at the base as they cover the ground and prevent weeds. This does work and you will hear people talk about this method, known as the three sister's method, which involves also planting climbing beans. The downside of this method is that the corn matures before the pumpkins so you can end up tiptoeing through the pumpkins carefully to harvest the corn, but if you don't mind that then this is a great way to make good use of space.

Look at your main crop, slow-maturing plants that you have planted, and don't just ignore the space between them. Use it for growing short-season crops and maximize your production!

Succession Planting

This strategy overcomes the problem many gardeners face of a glut of vegetables. When you plant a row of lettuce plants, they are all ready within a week or two of each other and you find you have more lettuce than you can use. The result is a lot of it bolts and becomes inedible, being discarded on the compost heap. Either that or you are giving away vegetables to everyone you know (I used to bring them into work and leave them on reception for anyone to take!).

By adopting the succession planting strategy, you ensure that you get a steady supply of short-season vegetables throughout the growing season and you avoid the glut problem.

Typically, you will plant a small patch of the short-season vegetable every two to three weeks throughout the growing season rather than planting lots all at once. Plants such as carrots, beets, green onions, cilantro, radishes, basils, arugula, spinach, and lettuce are all suitable for succession planting. As the plants mature, they are harvested and when they are spent the next planting should be ready to harvest. This method also means that if one planting is lost due to the weather or pests you haven't lost your entire crop.

For example, with lettuce, you would plant about an eighth of a teaspoon of seeds every two weeks and this will give you a steady supply throughout the growing season. An excess of produce is one of the main problems a gardener will face. It's fine if you have family and friends you can give it to, but you can find too much produce a little overwhelming.

This method doesn't work for longer season vegetables because they take so long to mature. These would typically be preserved or frozen if not used immediately when they are mature.

Trap Crops

This is a great planting strategy that involves planting a sacrificial crop. Garden pests are attracted to this crop which you then uproot and destroy once infested which knocks back the breeding population of that pest. If you live in an area that suffers from particular pests, then this could be a good strategy for growing vegetables that would otherwise be decimated by pests.

For example, nasturtiums are loved by aphids, so you would plant these near to your cabbages to draw the aphids away from your crop.

You then cover the sacrificial crop with a plastic bag, taking care the pests do not escape and then destroy it. Leaving the plant in the sealed bag in the sun will kill the pests or you can burn it. If you are putting this on your compost pile then you need to bury it in the middle of a hot compost pile otherwise the pests will survive and escape. As most of us do not run compost heaps hot enough to kill the pests, I would recommend destroying the infected plant material.

You can boost the population of beneficial insects by leaving a few of these trap plants away from your crop as the predators will remain in your vegetable plot and continue to hunt the pests.

Companion Planting

This is the practice of pairing together plants that help each other either by enhancing their growth or keeping away pests.

The corn/bean/squash method described above is a fine example of companion planting. The beans climb up the corn and fix nitrogen into the soil. The squash helps retain soil moisture as well as deter rodents and keep the weeds down.

Planting aromatic herbs around your vegetable beds, or even amongst them is another great way to confuse pests because they cannot detect your vegetable crops. Planting leeks, garlic or onions next to your carrots is another good example of this technique and will keep off carrot fly, which hunts by smell.

Companion planting is a very natural technique that works well and you should try planting basil and tomatoes together as the basil will enhance the flavor of the tomatoes! This is quite a complex subject, with a lot of great companions.

Chapter 5: How to Grow Vegetables in your Vegetable Gardening for Year-Round Growing

Growing your own vegetables is a very fun pastime, which also has many beneficial benefits such as healthy food (you know what additives were used if any), exercise, outdoor work etc. Growing your own vegetables is also a wonderful activity for the entire family to participate, as it helps kids understand better how nature works and where food comes from.

Some people think a lot of space is needed to grow your own vegetables. When you are trying to provide the family with a range of vegetables every day of the year, this is definitely real. It's not true if you cultivate your own vegetables to complement your grocery shopping to have some fresh vegetables. For example, four or so runner bean (Pole Bean) plants in a patio container should provide more than enough beans for a family of four for a few months.

When it comes to vegetables, each country in the world has different varieties that grow best in their specific climate, even in some countries a specific crop that grows well in one region does not grow at all in another as the climate and atmosphere are different. It's here where some of the fun comes into growing your own because you can experiment with different vegetable varieties from different parts of the world to see what you can and can't produce, experimentation will also be required to establish specific growing conditions for these unique varieties for your environment.

There are two ways to have our own gardens at home, in the external area (backyard) or in the internal area (kitchen, balcony, balcony, service area). Let's deal with the first way, which will probably be subject to the weather. The success of a vegetable garden, in this case, is directly related to the right moment of each planting of herbs, vegetables, and vegetables. Each month has its characteristics, which make them more suitable for each species.

The plants are different from each other concerning the type of soil and temperatures necessary for their full development, so it is very important to know what are the most suitable options for each season of the year.

Below, we have prepared a list of the most used plants in vegetable gardens and which month, or months, are most suitable for planting.

- January: lettuce, watercress, celery, various cabbages, radish, almond, turnip, beet, arugula, chicory, spinach, sweet potato, parsley, coriander, purslane, carrot, Brussels sprouts, and cabbage;

- February: watercress, lettuce, chicory, beans, parsley, radish, cabbage, beets, cabbage, peas, spinach, and beans;

- March: carrot, almond, parsley, garlic, lettuce, chicory, spinach, celery, miscellaneous cabbages, cauliflower, broccoli, cabbage, watercress, celery, onion, coriander, peas, beans, beans, strawberry, turnip, radish, and cabbage ;

- April: watercress, almond, beet, turnip, parsley, garlic, arugula, chicory, celery, cauliflower, broccoli, cabbage, spinach, carrot, coriander, pea, asparagus, broad bean, lentil, strawberry, radish, lettuce, onion, and various cabbages;

- May: radish, carrot, almond, turnip, beet, arugula, parsley, chicory, celery, spinach, cauliflower, broccoli, winter cabbage, garlic, lettuce, potato, onion, various cabbages, fava, and strawberry;

- June: almond, carrot, turnip, beet, arugula, garlic, chicory, watercress, cauliflower, broccoli and winter cabbage;

- July: pea, almond, arugula, garlic, lettuce, radish, chicory, beet, broad bean, and cabbage;

- August: artichoke, white celery, jiló, eggplant, various peppers, peppers, tomatoes, onion, cabbage, asparagus, strawberry, melon, watermelon, and cucumber;

- September: lettuce, radish, beet, carrot, miscellaneous cabbages, cauliflower, broccoli, jiló, eggplant, miscellaneous peppers, peppers, tomatoes, squash, zucchini, green beans, cucumber, gherkin, parsley, coriander, onion, peas, spinach, fava beans, lentils, melons, watermelons, and turnips;

- October: chard, carrot, various cabbages, cauliflower, broccoli, cabbage, various peppers, peppers, tomatoes, eggplant, jiló, pumpkin, zucchini, green beans, cucumber, gherkin, mandioquinha, parsley, potato, sweet potato, coriander, watercress, lettuce, beet, broccoli, chicory, cumin, broad bean, melon, watermelon, turnip, radish, thyme, onion, and tomato;

- November: pumpkin, watercress, lettuce, radish, carrot, broccoli, cabbage, various cabbages, cauliflower, sweet potato, coriander, beet, spinach, beans, melon, watermelon, turnip, cucumber, and various peppers;

- December: pumpkin, zucchini, green beans, cucumber, carrots, cabbage, watercress, lettuce, beets, broccoli, various cabbages, spinach, melon, watermelon, turnip, various peppers, and radish.

There are still many herbs that are considered perennial, produce all year round, such as sage, parsley, chives, marjoram, basil, for example, but that cannot resist very low temperatures or frosts, so, interestingly, they are planted in more protected places.

Another important point to note is the use of greenhouses; for example, some plants in greenhouses have their productivity extended for many more months.

The other option, mentioned above, of growing a vegetable garden indoors is ideal for those who live in apartments and dream of having an organic garden without pesticides. This can be done in pots and the location chosen for its location inside the house, allows you to decide less for the month of the year and more for the climate that we create in the indoor environment.

You can create light and temperature conditions for your favorite herbs. We have selected some garden options available for sale that can give you a good idea of how to build yours. They can stay in the kitchen, laundry area, on the balcony, in short, wherever there is space available for you to cultivate your new hobby.

Chapter 6: How to Grow Flowers, Fruits and Herbs in your Vegetable Gardening

Making use of raised garden beds for the cultivation of flowers may not appeal to everyone. After all, how many flowers can you eat?

However, the joy and interest that beautiful blooms bring to every garden cannot be denied.

Flowers also attract a variety of pollinators, among which is the much-maligned and seriously jeopardized honey bee.

Tara Nolan (2017), in her article, Tips for Planting and Making Raised Flower Beds, agrees that growing blooms alongside vegetables, herbs, and fruits have many advantages.

Careful planning of your raised bed floral garden can give rise to many hours of pleasure as well as plenty of bouquets of summer flowers to brighten your home and cheer neighbors and friends.

When planting from seeds, ensure you carefully note the requirements for each variety as well as their height at maturity. Taller plants should be placed towards the center of the raised bed, allowing more convenient access to the shorter flowers that you can plant around the edges.

Feeding your floral garden with proper nutrients and keeping it well hydrated is of the utmost importance. Mulching will keep the roots protected and ensure these do not dry out too quickly in warmer weather.

Nolan (2017) suggests sunflowers, zinnias, daylilies, and cosmos are easy to grow and produce an attractive show. Gladiolus and lilies may be successfully planted where there are no squirrels to decimate the bulbs.

Essential Aspects to Consider When Choosing Flowers

According to her article, 21 Easiest Flowers for Beginners, Linda Hagen (2019) suggests the following important points should be carefully considered as you set out to plan your new raised bed garden.

Take Careful Note of Your Garden Area

Consider the amount of available space you have for your raised garden beds. Get acquainted with the gardening site.

Take the position of the planned garden into consideration as well as whether there will be sufficient sunlight for your plants.

Check the type of soil in your area as well as its ability to hold water. Good soil quality will ensure healthy plant growth.

Know your frost cycle, and ensure you plant crops and flowers according to what will grow best in your zone.

Take a good look at the plants growing in your neighborhood. This will give you a good idea of what is likely to grow successfully in your new garden.

Choose Flowers to Suit Your Style

The same article suggests that although gardening can be a wonderfully therapeutic experience, beginners should remember to curb their enthusiasm for overindulging in too many colors and varieties of blooms. It is prudent to start off deciding on a basic color scheme that will suit your personality and style.

If you prefer a garden that whispers tranquillity and peace, choose flowers in shades of blue, purple, and soft pinks with a dash of white and yellow.

However, if your style leans to the more vibrant and exciting side, a mix of cheerful, brightly colored flowers may suit you better.

The recommendation in the same article by Garden Design Magazine (2019b) is to avoid too much variety, and colors that clash as this is likely to affect the overall beauty of your garden adversely.

Inventive Designs Catch the Imagination

Think fragrance, movement, color, and the overall final impact you would like your raised bed garden to have.

Piet Oudolf, the internationally renowned garden designer from the Netherlands, designs his gardens around the structure and shapes of the flowers he plants (Garden Design Magazine, 2019b). Piet suggests choosing blooms that have reliable, stout's stalks so that after they flower, these stems, topped by their attractive seed pods, will make a beautiful display when covered with snow.

Perennials come in a variety of shapes that include bells, spikes, plumes, screens, and buttons to name but a few.

Careful consideration of and inventive grouping of a variety of plant shapes will lead to pockets of interest and surprise in your new garden.

Plan on layering your flowers, so they blend as naturally as possible to create a free-flowing bank of gorgeous blooms.

Depending on the position of your raised bed garden, consider placing taller plants towards the center or back with plants of medium height next. The shorter, bushier plants should be placed towards the front and sides of the garden.

You can add objects such as a statue or a boulder or perhaps a birdbath to your raised bed garden. These items will create added interest and will encourage birds that are useful pollinators into this eco-friendly space.

Consider planting lots of foliage-producing plants as well if you intend to cultivate flowers for cutting (Garden Design Magazine, 2019b).

Fair Flowers for Floral Fragrance

Choosing flowers for your raised bed may be quite an overwhelming experience, to begin with. There are many different varieties available, each with specific characteristics of its own.

Some flowers are prized for their astonishingly beautiful colors, hues, and shades while others are chosen for their tall, majestic stems. Then there are those gorgeous blooms that enthral us with their enchanting fragrance.

Other flowers are valued for their medicinal properties, and others find favor in being the most suitable for bordering your raised beds in cheerful abundance.

In her article, 21 Easiest Flowers for Beginners, Hagen (2019) suggests a wide variety of easy-to-grow flowers for any beginner gardener to enjoy. Among these, she includes the following suitable annuals that will be suitable for raised garden beds:

Dianthus

ZONE: 3-9

These showy, fragrant flowers surrounded by lush, evergreen foliage bloom from May to August and grow to a height of about 20 inches.

They flourish in well-drained soil and require small amounts of water, preferring not to become water-logged.

Dianthus grow well in either full sun or semi-shade. These small, colorful flowers are resistant to deer and will bring gorgeous splashes of color to your raised bed garden.

Fuchsias

ZONE: Annual, everywhere except for 10-11

The Fuchsias' gorgeous shades of pink, magenta, purple, lavender and white make for attractive displays, ideal for hanging baskets on patios or in trees where they thrive in shady spots.

These lovely plants prefer moist, well-drained soil and require regular pruning to attract new growth. They attract hummingbirds, bees, and butterflies.

Fuchsias grown in Southern California and Bay Areas are prone to fuchsia mites.

Geraniums

ZONE: 10-11 (Grown as an annual everywhere else)

These hardy, sun-loving plants that enjoy fertile, well-drained soil are ideal for raised bed gardens.

Geraniums come in a variety of shades from magenta through red, pink, lavender, and white.

These plants can reach heights of 24 inches when mature. They attract birds, bees, and butterflies.

Lupines

ZONE: 4-8 where they are often grown as an annual

Lupines are tall, quite majestic plants that can reach a height of four feet.

These happy, little flowers enjoy being in the full sun in colder climates and partial shade in warmer areas. They are attractive to butterflies.

Lupins come in a variety of gorgeous blues, lavenders, and pinks. There are white and yellow varieties as well. They grow well from seed and are good self-sowers.

These plants require a good, deep soaking but their roots must be allowed to dry out between watering.

Morning Glories

ZONE: Annual

Morning glories love the full sun and bloom late summer or early in the fall. These climbers in shades of blue, purple, white, and pink make excellent plants for trellis covers and readily self-sow.

Although these plants attract butterflies as well as birds, the seeds are highly poisonous if eaten.

Morning glories prefer fertilized, well-drained soil and require regular watering during dry periods.

Pansies

ZONE: 6-10 grown as perennials/biennials

Pansies are ideal plants for warmer areas where they will bloom throughout the winter and well into early spring.

The plants prefer well-fertilized, well-drained soils and require regular watering. They enjoy sunny conditions but will also thrive in partial shade.

Pansies come in a variety of attractive colors and grow to a maximum height of nine inches.

Snapdragon

ZONE: Annuals everywhere except for 5-10 where they grow as perennials

These attractive 6-15 inch tall plants come in a variety of lovely colors from white, pink, and lavender to red, orange, and peach.

Snapdragons will enjoy a sunny spot in your garden and will bloom from spring through fall. These interestingly-shaped flowers attract butterflies.

They require well-drained, fertile soil and regular watering.

Sunflowers

ZONE: Annual

These cheerful, yellow flowers grow to a height of between 3 and 16 feet. Because of their height and their brittle stems, to ensure your sunflowers remain upright, it is prudent to place supports into the ground for these plants.

They are tough plants that cope well in most soil types and are drought resistant, so they require less water than other plants.

Sunflowers do best in full sun and bloom during the summer. They attract bees, butterflies, and some seed-eating birds.

Sunflowers make a great backdrop in a garden or as a cut flower.

Sweet Peas

ZONE: Annual

These wonderfully scented plants come in a variety of colors and make an attractive addition to any garden.

They prefer regular watering in good-quality loamy soil that is well-drained.

Sweet peas do well in full sun and can be successfully grown on a trellis as their soft stems require added support.

Zinnias

ZONE: Annual

These summer bloomers that grow well in full sunlight come in a variety of shades of red, orange, yellow, white, and some pinks.

Although zinnias are relatively hardy plants, they prefer more fertile soil that drains well. Their water requirements are minimal.

Zinnias bloom during the summer and can reach a height of about 24 inches. They are, therefore, suitable flowers for cutting as their long, sturdy stems look good in a vase.

Chapter 7: What are the Tools and Equipment You Need

Many of all the things that you need are likely already around your home -- mainly if you're working on other outside jobs.

Here's a brief list of some Helpful gardening equipment:

1.   Gloves allow you to grasp resources better and assist you to avert hand blisters. Cotton gloves would be the most affordable, but the expensive creature skin lotions -- made of sheep and goatskin, such as -- persist more.

2.   An excellent straw hat with venting retains the Sunshine off your skin and allows air to move through and cool your mind.

3.   An excellent pocketknife or set of pruning shears is excellent for cutting edge strings and blossoms.

4.   Sturdy rubber boots, garden clogs, or function Boots repel water and supply aid for digging.

5.   Bug repellent and sunscreen keep you Comfy and secure while working in the garden.

6.   Watering Hoses and Cans

Plants need water to grow, and when Mother Nature is not cooperating, you want to water frequently. For a vast garden, you might require fancy soaker hoses, sprinklers, and drip irrigation pipes. However, for many small house gardeners, a straightforward hose and watering can perform. Rubber hoses are a lesser chance to kink than nylon or plastic pads, but they usually are much heavier to maneuver around. Whatever material you choose, make sure you acquire a hose that is long enough to achieve plants in every area of your garden without needing to take water round the beds to complete distant plants. Decide on a hose which includes brass fittings and a washer incorporated to the tube; those components make the machine not as likely to fail after prolonged usage. Watering cans can be made from natural, cheap, brightly colored plastic or high end, fancy metal. Vinyl is lighter, but galvanized metal is rustproof and much more appealing. Watering cans come in various sizes, so try several out for relaxation before purchasing. Ensure it is simple to eliminate the sprinkler head, or improved, for cleanup.

7. Hand Trowels

Hand Trowels are crucial for digging in containers, window boxes, and little raised beds. The wider-bladed hand trowels that can be brightly shaped and round the conclusion, are simpler to use to loosen dirt compared to narrower bladed, V-pointed ones, these thinner blades are better for grinding tough weeds, like dandelions.

8. Hand Cultivators

A three-pronged hand cultivator is a useful tool to split up dirt clods, Straight forward seedbeds, and also operate in granular fertilizer. Additionally, once you plant your little container or elevated foundation, the weeds will come if you want it or not a cultivator functions as a fantastic tool to eliminate these youthful weeds as they germinate. When you are digging a planting hole, then a hand cultivator divides the ground more readily compared to a hand trowel. Much like a hand trowel, make sure to opt for a hand cultivator that feels comfortable on your hands which includes a grip firmly fastened to the blade. The steel-bladed kinds will be the most lasting.

9. Spades and Shovels

Lo Spades and shovels are just two of the most widely used gardening gear. The gap between both is straightforward: A spade is created for grinding, and a spade was created for scooping and projecting. Shovels traditionally have curved and pointed blades, whereas spades possess flat, right, nearly rotating blades. A fantastic spade is vital in any garden for distributing dirt, manure, or compost. A shovel is crucial for trimming or breaking fresh ground. But many gardeners use spades for whatever from cutting dirt luggage to hammering in bets. Very good spades are rocky. The two spades and shovels arrive in brief - and - long-handled versions. An extended handle gives you more leverage when digging holes, so bear this in mind if you are buying a new spade.

10. Garden Forks

Useful since a spade is for turning new garden dirt, I find an iron fork is a much better instrument for turning beds which were worked before. The fork slips to the ground as deep as 12 inches, and in precisely the same time divides clods and loosens and aerates the soil more significant than a shovel. Iron forks look very similar to short-handled spades except they have three to four iron tines in their heads. The top ones will be those forged from 1 piece of steel with wood grips firmly attached. They are great not just for turning dirt but also for turning compost piles and smelling root crops, like carrots and potatoes.

11. Garden Rakes

When you dig soil, you have to level it, Split dirt clods, and eloquent that the seedbeds (particularly if you're climbing beds that are raised). An iron rake is an ideal tool for the job though you can use it for this purpose just a few times annually. A 14-inch-diameter, iron-toothed rake ought to have a long, wooden handle that is securely attached to a metallic head. You may turn the metallic head to smooth a seedbed level. To get a lightweight but less lasting version of an iron rake, then try out an aluminium rake.

12. Buckets, Wagons, also Baskets

You do not possess a 1,000-square-foot garden. However, you still should carry seeds, fertilizer, tools, create, and other things around. I enjoy speaking about storage containers since this is where the means of this trade get very straightforward. Listed below are three original containers:

✓ Buckets: For potting soil, fertilizers, and hand tools, a 5-gallon plastic bucket is the best container. You are likely to get one free in the building site: be sure that you wash it out nicely. To get a more durable but smaller bucket, then purchase one made out of galvanized steel.

✓ Wagons: For lighter things, like apartments of seedlings, use a kid's old red wagon. Wagons are fantastic for transferring plants and tiny bags of compost in your garden, along with the lip to the wagon bed, helps maintain these things in place when you pay bumpy ground. If you are considering a wagon to maneuver yourself (rather than just gear) around the garden, innovation is a saddle using a chair. This sort of wagon generally has a swivelling chair and can be perched on four analog wheels, letting you sit down and push yourself throughout the garden as you operate. Its storage space under the chair too.

✓ Baskets: To collect that entire fantastic make you develop and harvest, put money into a cable or wicker basket. Wire baskets are more comfortable to use as it is possible to wash the produce while it's still from the basket, wicker and wooden baskets, even though more durable than steel, are more aesthetically pleasing and trendy on your garden. Piling your crate in a basket is much more functional than attempting to balance zucchinis on your arms while taking them out of the garden to your kitchen.

13. Wheelbarrows and Garden Carts

Invariably you have to move heavy things like dirt and fertilizer from 1 place to another in your lawn or garden. The two chief choices for transferring stuff that is "bigger than a bread box" are wheelbarrows and garden carts. The simple difference between the two vehicles would be that the wheels. Wheelbarrows have a single bike along with an oval, alloy tray; garden packs have two wheels and a rectangular wooden tray. Wheelbarrows are maneuverable in tight areas, can flip on a dime, and are simple to dump. A contractor-type wheelbarrow has a deeper box also is well worth the excess investment due to its exceptional quality. To get a lightweight wheelbarrow, try one with a table made from plastic. Garden carts are much better, can carry bigger loads, and are easier to drive than wheelbarrows. A larger-sized garden cart can easily manage loads of dirt, dirt, stone, and bales of hay. Some garden carts have detachable rear panels which make dumping simpler.

14. Power Tillers

The classic back - or front-tined power tiller was developed to aid large-scale anglers to save time turning their gardens in autumn and spring. The large power tillers (higher than a 5-horsepower motor) are greatest if you have 1,000 square feet or longer to until. Additionally, they can be crucial tools for forming raised beds and dividing sod.

Chapter 8: Hydroponics Gardening

A straightforward definition of hydroponics is a way to grow plants in a nutrient-rich, water-based solution. It doesn't use any dirt or soil. The logic behind hydroponics is letting the roots of the plants to come in contact with the solution that is full of nutrients. The plants also have access to plenty of oxygen that the plants need to grow correctly.

The root system of the plants won't have as much stress when they are grown in these types of environments since they don't have to find food from the soil, and they can convert the nutrients into energy a lot faster. This will result in more excellent products in a short amount of time.

Since plants are grown without soil, you have to maximize the root's nutrient absorption. This means the way you give the roots their nutrients is extremely important.

This system could be either passive or active. Passive meant that there aren't any moving parts and you are going to have to use some electricity. A dynamic system means that nutrients are given by using a pump. There are some variations to these types of systems, which means that a passive system could incorporate a pump, but this isn't common.

Another aspect of this system is characterized by the non-recovery or recovery of the nutrients. There are specific systems that use a solution just one time, and then it gets thrown away.

A recovery system recirculates the nutrient solution. Even though the non-recovery system is better cost-wise, it could be harmful if you are growing a large number of plants because it compromises hygiene.

Hydroponics has had a place in various civilizations throughout history. The floating gardens in China and Mexico, along with the hanging gardens in Babylon, are a few examples of hydroponic culture. Hieroglyphics found in Egypt date back to many hundreds of years BC. They talk about growing plants in water. Even though hydroponics is an ancient way to grow plants, there have been significant strides made through the years to this part of agriculture.

During the past century, horticulturists and scientists have been experimenting with various hydroponic ways. One hydroponic application that has caused more research was growing fresh produce in places where crops wouldn't normally grow. Hydroponics was used in World War II to give troops who were stationed on various islands in the Pacific where food wouldn't increase with produce they were able to improve themselves.

Later in that same century, hydroponics was put into use by the space program. While NASA was talking about trying to put people on other planets or even the moon, hydroponics fit into their plans quickly. By 1970, analysts and scientists weren't the only ones who were involved in hydroponics. Hobbyists and farmers began to be attracted to the ways of hydroponics.

Place take the time to read through this whole guide and do some research on your own so you can learn all you can learn about hydroponics before you ever begin your garden. Even if you don't want to grow plants using hydroponics, you can still learn about all the different plants and what they need during various stages of their life by reading about hydroponics.

Benefits

The primary purpose of using a hydroponic system is giving the plant the three essential things that it needs to grow correctly, and these are light, nutrients, and water. In the right conditions, when these things are met, plants will become strong, healthy, and produce a high yield.

If the perfect conditions aren't met, the plants are going to suffer, and the yield won't be as high. The plants are going to be weak, and the product will be of bad quality.

There are some drawbacks and benefits to setting up a hydroponic system. Before you decide on one order, you need to ask yourself a few questions:

- How much budget?

- What type of experience do I have?

- Am I growing commercially or for personal use?

- How large of a space do I have?

- What do I want to grow; flowers, medicinal, or food?

- How much time do I have daily?

Starting with a small setup just for your pleasure can be fun, affordable, rewarding, and above all, natural. By using hydroponics, you will be creating the perfect environment for your plants. If plants are grown without soil, there won't be as much stress on the roots. They don't have to search for nutrients since you are already giving the plants everything they need.

There are some benefits to growing plants using hydroponics. Some of these include:

- Not needing to use pesticides since the majority of all pests live in the soil. This makes our food, water, land, and air so much cleaner.

- Being able to grow a lot of food better than conventional agriculture that only uses soil.

- Growing foods in places that can't support growing plants in healthy soil.

Let's look at this in more detail. When you grow plants in a hydroponic system that has been set up the right way, it is going to increase the growth rate of your plants. They are going to mature about 25 percent faster and are going to produce about 30 percent more product than plants that are grown in healthy soil.

Plants will have the ability to grow larger and faster since they don't have to work to find the nutrients they need. Even the smallest roots are going to give the plant all it needs to survive and thrive. This allows the plant to focus on growing the plant's body instead of growing its roots to find nutrients.

All of this is possible as long as you can control the pH and nutrient solutions levels. Hydroponics uses less water than plants that are grown in the soil since the system is enclosed, and evaporation doesn't happen as often. It might be hard to believe, but hydroponics is a lot better for our environment because it reduces pollution and waste from the soil runoff.

Although the benefits of growing food by using a hydroponic system have been well documented, and there are a lot of them, commercial growers are still very reluctant to embrace hydroponics. The main reason is that governments across the world still think of hydroponics as a way only to grow marijuana. The government always persecutes any company that uses hydroponics. As time goes by, concerns about our environment and having less land to grow plants will bring on global awareness about all the advantages of hydroponics for home gardeners and farmers, too.

Some commercial growers are embracing hydroponics. The ideals that surround this type of growing system talk about subjects many people are passionate about like making our world cleaner and ending world hunger. People from all over the world have bought hand are building their system. They want to grow fresh, wonderful-tasting foods for their friends and family. People are making their dreams come true by having their own business of growing produce that they can sell to local restaurants and at farmer's markets. Educators realize all the various applications that hydroponics have and are teaching their students about the science behind this type of gardening.

Hydroponic research is increasing as all the numerous benefits are being realized. Other types of systems like aquaponics and aeroponics are leading the way, and we have no idea of what the future holds for these types of technologies. We do know that hydroponics continues to drive innovation and give us more cutting edge resources and techniques.

Soil Gardening Versus Hydroponics

As stated above, hydroponics is a gardening system that doesn't use soil. Plants are put into a growing medium, and nutrients are given to the roots. Most people get surprised when they are told that plants don't need soil to survive. Soil can be an inefficient growing medium. Plants use a lot of their energy growing roots so they can find the nutrients they need to survive. When you give them readily available and constant nutrition, hydroponics let plants grow about 50 percent faster than they will in soil.

There are many benefits to gardening without soil:

· You can grow food all year long.

· It's a great way to spend some quality time with family.

· You have complete control over the level of nutrients you use.

· A small hydroponic garden is more productive than more extensive gardens.

· Most people say gardening with hydroponics is very relaxing.

· You can make a hydroponic system in any size of indoor space.

· You can be sure of having success when grown with hydroponics.

· Hydroponics use about 2.3 less water than typical gardens.

· Hydroponics gives you better tasting and more nutritious foods.

· It is very affordable. You can get started on a minimal budget and can save a lot of money no matter what size your project is.

Disadvantages

Despite all the advantages that a hydroponic system can give you, there are some disadvantages, too. The largest one is that even though most people say they are affordable; in the beginning, it can be quite expensive to purchase every aspect you need to create a hydroponic system. If you don't have any experience with this type of policy, you might be successful in your first few tries. When you consider that soil usually doesn't cost you anything, but you do get what you pay for.

If you decide to go with an extensive system, it could take some time to set up if you aren't an experienced gardener. Managing your order is going to take some time, too. You are going to have to monitor and balance the nutrient and pH levels daily.

The most significant risk of a hydroponic system is the smallest thing, such as a pump failure could kill your plants in a manner of hours according to the size of the system. The plants could die very fast since the growing medium isn't able to store the water like soil can. These plants depend on having a fresh supply of water at all times.

Chapter 9: Hydroponics vs. Soil Gardening

Both hydroponic and soil gardening methods have their advantages and disadvantages, and as you will discover that not all plants are suitable for hydroponic systems. However, a surprising number are, including many that you would not think could be grown without soil, such as potatoes and carrots.

Areas Where Hydroponic Gardening is better than Soil Gardening

Hydroponics save Space

Hydroponic takes up very little space, and you can grow an indoor hydroponic system in your room. Besides, the absence of soil means root systems are short, so you can grow plants closer together and save space.

Weather free growing

The weather can be the biggest hindrance to growing anything outside. In a hydroponic system, you have full control over the environment and are growing indoors, so there is no weather to upset your growing plans!

Lower water use

Growing in soil is surprisingly water inefficient, so in an area where water is expensive or scarce, it is very costly to grow vegetables. However, a hydroponic system, despite being made up mainly of water, using significantly less water than growing in soil because it is more efficient in its use of water.

Fewer pests

Have you ever lost your crop to pests? Had caterpillars devoured your cauliflower? Pests are a significant problem when growing outside and mean either companion planting, using the pesticide, or accepting you will lose a portion of your crop. Hydroponic plants are grown indoors in an enclosed environment, so the chances of pests are meager. Of course, there is the chance that you will find the occasional pest, but as you are regularly checking the system, you tend to spot any pest problems very early on before they cause much damage.

Fewer diseases

It is very frustrating to lose your entire crop because of a disease. Although you can spray for many conditions, there are just as many for which there is no treatment. As you are growing indoors, diseases are very uncommon. Practicing proper hygiene and quarantining new plants before introducing them to the system will help to reduce the risk of illness to virtually zero.

Fewer artificial chemicals

Although there is a significant movement away from the use of chemicals in gardening, they are still introduced into your garden through the wind and rain. However, some gardeners will use pesticides and artificial fertilizers. Growing hydroponically, you use far fewer chemicals, which is a huge benefit for many gardeners.

No digging

A distaste of many gardeners is the need to dig over the soil, hence the popularity of systems such as the no-dig system involving layering compost and cardboard. There is no digging involved in hydroponic gardening, as there is no soil.

Rapid maturing crops

When you grow plants hydroponically, they mature far faster than if they are grown in soil or even in a greenhouse. Typically, plants will develop in three-quarters of the usual growing time, but some can mature in up to half the time. This means you can get more crops per year, and when combined with the next point, has significant benefits for commercial growers.

Reliable & predictable yields

Growing hydroponically produces very reliable yields because you are not reliant on the vagrancies of the weather. Yields are typically much higher because of the consistent growing conditions, producing up to double the yield.

Lower labor requirement

Because there is less work involved, you just check the pH and nutrient levels regularly, there is a lot less labor involved.

Higher nutritional content

Scientific analysis of hydroponically grown vegetables has shown that they contain up to 50% more vitamins and minerals than vegetables grown in soil. This means some health benefits and is a big advantage for many growers.

Hydroponics uses less water

When grown via a hydroponic system, the plants need less water. When you water plants that are in the soil, often the water seeps into the ground, and some water also gets evaporated. But the hydroponic system is much more water-efficient, and you use 70 to 80% less water.

Hydroponics systems lower, pests, weeds, and diseases

With traditional soil planting the risk of pests, weeds, and diseases increases; but a hydroponic system deals with this problem almost completely.

Hydroponic systems grow plants faster

Hydroponic systems grow plants twice as fast as traditional methods, which means you get more harvests every year. The growing cycle is much more efficient because the plants get everything it needs.

Hydroponics let you adjust nutrient content for different plants

Hydroponics allows you to tweak and adapt nutrients for every plant.

Areas Where Soil Gardening is better

Lower initial cost

The initial cost of hydroponics can be quite expensive. But soil gardening has a lower initial price.

No need to use electricity

A light source is needed in several hydroponic gardening techniques. Also, some systems use power to aerate the roots.

Less risk of bacteria and mold growth

In a hydroponics system, plants grow in a very moist environment. If precautions are not taken, then there is a susceptible risk of mold and bacteria growth.

Now you know the main differences between the traditional soil growing method and the hydroponics system.

Chapter 10: Setting Up Your Hydroponic Garden

Useful Strategies for Growing Plants inside Hydroponically

Here are a couple of additional strategies and factors to keep in your mind for the new garden:

- Lighting: Merely because a plant has been growing in water does not necessarily indicate it does not still require sun. Particularly in the case of vegetables and fruits such as tomatoes and many anything with blossoms, you will have to either put your plants close to a south-facing window or even find out another method to receive them much-needed mild -- preferably at least half hours every day. Sadly, this is sometimes very complex due to several spectrums of intensity, light, and electricity, and of course different demands of various plants.

- PH Level: based on what you are attempting to increase, not getting the best pH level of your water may greatly reduce your crops' capacity to absorb carbohydrates, carbs, and other nutritional supplements. (as an example, the majority of the herbs mentioned previously flourish in a pH level which is lower compared to that of tap water) So it is important to look at the perfect pH tastes of your crops and fix the water so.

- Climate/Temperature: since most crops prefer a temperature between 60--80°F, it is very important to keep a watch on how cold or hot it gets around your hydroponic garden. At times you will have to shield it in the warmth generated from the expansion lamps or a nearby radiator. Other times you will have to safeguard them from falling temperatures in winter, though they're inside.

What Is The Nutrient Film Technique (NFT)?

Nutrient Film Technique (NFT) is an energetic hydroponics system in which water containing dissolved nutrients is pumped into an increased menu, so those nutrients can be absorbed by plants because the water moves through their origins. This water is then emptied into a lower reservoir has been finally pumped straight back through the increased tray.

It is among the most versatile and popular methods for hydroponics and may be especially helpful for fast-paced, lightweight plants such as lettuce--although it isn't quite as powerful for developing thicker crops like berries.

Pick the Location

Find the hydroponic method within an encased arrangement, for example, a toddler or the cellar of your house, or in an outside deck or yard. The floor ought to be level to make sure consideration of enhancements and water to the crops at the computer system. If placing the machine out, protect the construction from the components, for example, providing a cinch hindrance, and inspect the water levels more commonly because of water episode out of evaporating. During cold temperatures, then bring the hydroponic construction indoors. If placing the machine in an interior room of your house, add produce lights to offer additional lighting into the crops.

- **Stage 1 Enhancements make a means through barrels by water drive**

Collect the Hydroponic System

The system entails six generating barrels made from 6" PVC pipe, also a rack alone and trellis made from PVC, also a 50-gallon nutritional dispenser, a siphon and also a complicated. The tank stays beneath the desk of 6" PVC making chambers, along with the siphon stays within the tank to induce up supplements to the crops by means to get a composite of diminutive PVC stations and

66

vinyl chambers. Each producing room has a drainpipe which contributes back into the tank. The complex sits across the stations and transmits pressurized water into the chambers. To acquire the improvements to the plants within this arrangement, water has been pushed through a square of PVC, the more complicated, and then gets taken out to nominal plastic chambers which continue running indoors all the larger creating chambers. The improvement chambers have small openings in them, 1 gap between each plant website. The improvements take the opening out and scatter the plant origins. At precisely the same time, the explosion of water leaves air bubbles so that the plants get sufficient oxygen.

- **Stage 2 Tank holds approximately 50 gallons of water**

Mix Both the Nutrients and Water in the Tank

Fill the 50-gallon tank. By then add 2 cups of improvements into the container (or as recommended by the compost mark), twist onto the siphon and allow the system continues operating for about 30 minutes to capture the majority of the improvements out and outside combined.

- **Stage 3 Insert Plants into the Growing Tubes**

Presumably, the very direct strategies to take care of plant a hydroponic nursery would be to utilize gotten seedlings, particularly if you don't have the opportunity to develop the seeds. The crucial thing is to decide on the most precious plants you can locate and then eliminate the majority of the ground off their concealed establishments. To wash off the dirt from the roots, then submerge the main ball into a bucket of warm to cool water. Water that's unreasonably hot or cold can deliver the plant to daze. Gently spare the roots to acquire the dirt outside. Any ground left to the roots can end up the small sprinkle holes at the improvement tubes.

After the roots are pristine, pull the equal amount of origins from you can throughout the bottom of this planting cup plus a brief time afterwards add stretched out dirt stones to maintain the plant setup and upstanding. The sandstones are tough, and they're amazingly light with the aim they don't damage the plant origins.

- **Stage 4 Tie the Plants into the Trellis**

Use the plant grabs and rope to permeate the plants into the trellis. The series provides them exemptions to grow up, which expands the distance in this maintained zone. Tie the series unreservedly into the most notable intention of the trellis, connect fastens and chain into the bottom of each plant, and closely wind the hints of the plants across the series.

- **Stage 5 Switch on the Vacuum and Monitor the System Daily**

Assess the water measures step by step; in particular areas, it could be crucial to test it several times every day, determined by water hardship due to unnecessary warmth and dispersal. Check the pH and nutritional supplements amounts as anticipated. Considering that the toaster runs complete-time, you should not waste time using a clock, nevertheless, guarantee that the tank does not dry out and also even the clot will burst into flames.

- **Stage 6 Plants will cover layout farther down the middle a month**

Screen Plant Growth

A large part of a month in the aftermath of planting and the crops will cover the trellis because they will have each of the enhancements and water they will need to grow fast. It is essential to keep a lookout for plant development and tie or fix the plant stalks in regular interims.

- **Stage 7 Check for Pests and Diseases**

Quest for indicators of diseases and pests, for example, the closeness of insect annoys, little leaves and foliar contaminations.

One debilitated plant could quickly spoil different ones as they're so near one another. Eliminate any cleared plants out instantly. Since plants climbed hydroponically do not need to devote their own imperativeness faking to locate sustenance, they could contribute more energy creating. This urges them to become valuable and much more comfortable considering the manner they can utilize a little essentialness to stop contaminations. Because the leaves of these plants never become moist besides around the off possibility it rains, they are broadly less likely to acquire foliage animal, shape and development.

Despite the manner that hydroponic crops are amazing at fighting ailments, however, they need to fight germs. Despite whether it is high-value, bugs and caterpillars could from by locating a path to the nursery. Pick off and eliminate any bugs that you visit.

Chapter 11: Equipment needed

PH meter

PH is a measure of how acidic or how alkaline water is. A pH of 7 is neutral. pH levels that range from 1 to 6 are acidic, and levels from 8 to 14 are considered alkaline or basic.

Different plants have their preferences regarding pH levels. To ensure the best possible growth, you need to have a way of testing and then adjusting the pH level of your water.

For example:

- Cabbage likes pH levels of 7.5
- Tomatoes like a pH of 6-6.5
- Sweet potatoes like a pH of 5.2-6
- Peppers like a pH of 5.5-7
- Lettuce and broccoli like a pH of 6-7

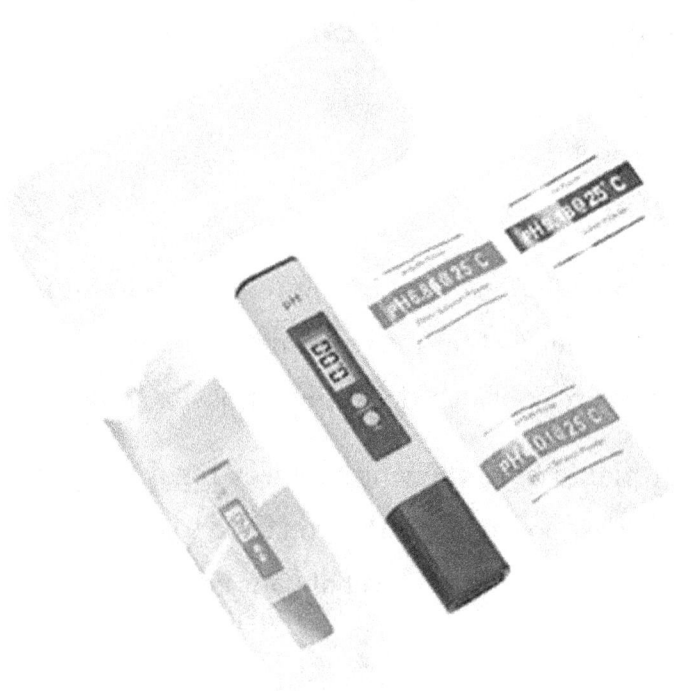

A basic pH meter

Don't use paper test strips for the water because they are inaccurate. Most of the time, a pH meter is offered in combination with a TDS or EC meter, which we will talk about next.

EC meter

Electrical conductivity is a measurement of how easily electricity passes through the water, the higher the ion content, the better it is at conducting electricity.

All water has ions in it. When you add nutrients to the water, you are increasing the ion content, effectively increasing the electrical conductivity.

EC or Electrical Conductivity is an integral part of the hydroponics equation. The simplest way of explaining this is as a guide to salts dissolved in water. Its unit is siemens per meter, but in hydroponics, we use millisiemens per meter.

In short, the higher the number of salts in the water, the higher the conductivity. Water that has no salt (distilled water) will have zero conductivity.

Lettuce likes an EC of 1.2 (or 1.2 millisiemens), while basil likes an EC of 2.

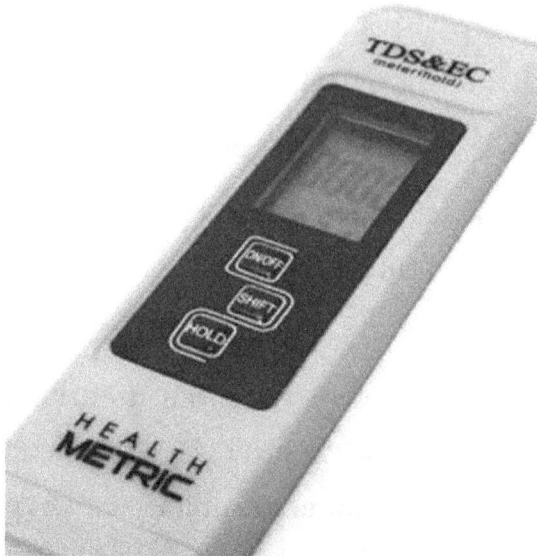

TDS & EC meter

That is why it is so important to know your EC and what your plants prefer, it will help you to ensure your system is at the right level.

However, electrical conductivity needs are also affected by the weather. When it is hot, the plants evaporate more water.

That is why you need to decrease the EC in hot summer months. In colder winter months, you need to increase the EC.

- In warm weather, you need to decrease the EC.
- In cold weather, you need to increase the EC.

TDS meter

TDS stands for total dissolved salts. You may hear some hydroponics growers referring to the TDS and not EC. These are both used to determine the strength of your hydroponic solution. If you buy a TDS meter, there will also be an option to switch to EC readings.

TDS readings are converted from an EC reading. The problem occurs when you don't know which calculation method was used to produce the TDS; there are several different ones.

In general, EC and CF readings are used in Europe, while TDS is an American measurement. But, regardless of which measurement you choose to use, they are both effectively the same thing: a measure of the nutrient levels in your solution.

The NaCl Conversion factor

This is effectively measuring salt in the water. The conversion factor for this mineral is your micro siemens figure multiplied by any number between 0.47 and 0.5. You'll find most TDS meters use 0.5. This is the easiest one for you to remember and calculate. Most of the meters sold will use the NaCl conversion factor.

As an example, if you have a reading of 1 EC (1 milli Siemens or 1000 micro Siemens), you will have a TDS reading of 500ppm.

Natural Water Conversion factor

This conversion factor is referred to as the 4-4-2; this quantifies its contents. Forty percent sodium sulfate, forty percent sodium bicarbonate, and twenty percent sodium chloride.

Again, the conversion factor is a range, this time between 0.65 and 0.85. Most TDS meters will use 0.7.

For example, 1 EC (1000 micro Siemens) will be 700 ppm with a TDS meter that uses the natural water conversion.

Potassium Chloride, KCl Conversion factor

This conversion factor is not a range this time. It is simply a figure of 0.55. Your EC meter reading 1EC or 1000 micro Siemens will equate to 550 ppm.

These are not all the possible conversion options, but they are the most common. The first, NaCl is the most used today.

Dissolved oxygen sensor

If plants don't get enough oxygen to their roots, they can die. A minimum of 5 ppm is recommended.

You do not need to invest in one if you oxygenate the water. Oxygenation of the water can be done by using an air pump with an airstone in the water tank. Depending on the method of growing, you don't need to aerate the water.

The dissolved oxygen in the water will be at its lowest during the summer. The water heats up, and the dissolved oxygen becomes less available. While your plants can do very well in winter, they might lack oxygen during summer.

Net Pots

Make sure you get the net pots with a lid on top to keep them from falling through. The standard size for lettuce is two inches (five centimeters). If you want to use tomatoes with dutch buckets, six inches (fifteen centimeters) is recommended.

3-Inch   **2-Inch**

3 and 2-inch (7 and 5 cm) net pots

If you are creating a new system on a budget, there are a variety of other options that can be used instead of buying net pots. For example, plastic cups with lots of holes in them, or simply fine netting on a wireframe. Use your imagination!

Humidity and Temperature Sensor

Estimating temperatures and humidity levels will lead to mistakes. I recommend getting a simple humidity and temperature sensor, so you don't need to guess. Most of them will cost you no more than $15.

Accurate humidity and temperature sensor

Germination tray and dome

You need to start seeds in a dedicated germination tray.

Most of these trays are 10x10 or 10x20 inches (25x25 or 25x50 centimeters) and generally include a humidity dome.

These trays are used to let your seeds germinate and keep the humidity high. After the first true leaves appear, it is time to transplant them into your system. Usually, this is after ten to fifteen days.

A 10x10 germination tray with a humidity dome

Seed Starter Cubes

If you are growing plants from seed, you can't simply place seeds in the net pots. They'll get washed away or sink. Instead, you need a seed starter cube. These cubes provide a place for the seed to start growing roots and flourish, safely.

Several materials can be used as your grow media when starting seeds:

Two seed starting cubes sheets

You can separate each cube from the bigger sheet. I recommend using gloves for this because the rock wool can be irritating on the skin.

As with every seed starter cube, you must soak it in pH neutral water of six before using it. This ensures that the seed has better germination rates.

Coco Coir

An alternative to rock wool cubes is coco coir. This is simply the fibrous coat of a coconut.

Coco coir is sold in briquettes

Coco coir is an organic media which will break down over time. Some people use it because it is environmentally friendly and renewable. I don't recommend it to start with. It can break down and clog your system if you are not careful. It can begin to rot somewhere, and before you know it, make your water quality terrible.

Sponges

Sponges are used most of the time as a cheap alternative to rock wool or oasis cubes. However, they do not absorb or retain moisture that well. That is why using sponges is not a carefree method of seed starting. They are not as environmentally friendly as the other seed starting cubes.

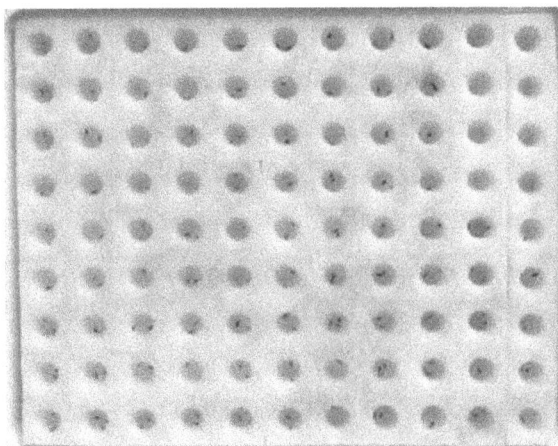

Seed starting sponges

Hydroton

This is the most popular growing media.

Hydroton is very lightweight, ensuring your pots aren't under any undue stress. It is excellent to keep your seed starter cubes in place. It's also easy on the hands and is pH neutral.

Hydroton

Chapter 12: Type of Systems

1. Hydroponic Drip Systems

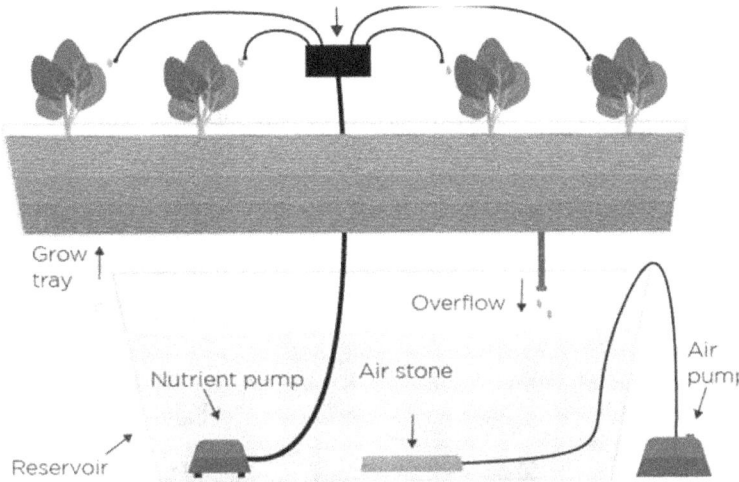

Drip systems are one of the most commonly utilized hydroponic systems in the country for both domestic farmers and company farmers. It is mostly because the principle is simple and needs a few components, but yet it is a rather diversified and efficient hydroponic method. While this is a simple idea, when designing your own structures, it won't hinder your creativity. The way a drip device operates, it allows you to spray nutritional substances on the roots of the plants to hold them moist.

Hydroponic drip systems can be conveniently built from tiny to large systems in several respects. But particularly useful for larger plants with plenty of root room. That is because you don't have to fill the network with vast amounts of water, and the drip lines are quick to extend over larger spaces. Besides using more growing media for larger plants, more growing media retains more moisture than smaller volumes, mainly because it is more forgiving for the plants.

Forgiving that the plants are not as prone to watering hours, and they do not automatically worry whether they are watered on time for one purpose or the other.

2. Ebb and Flow - (Flood And Drain) System

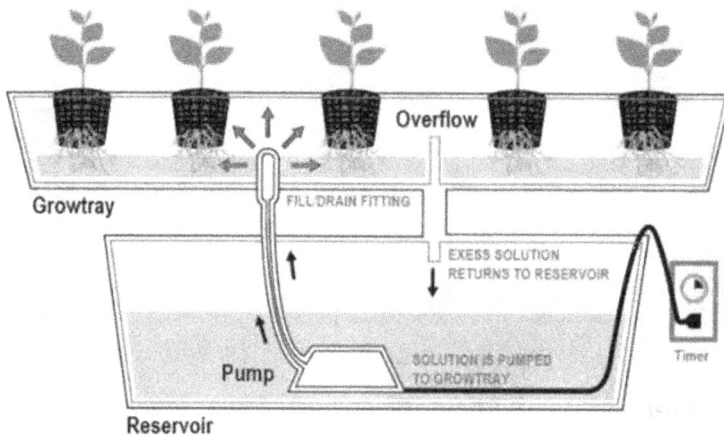

For several purposes, flood and drain systems (ebb and flow) are quite conventional with hydroponic farmers. You can construct them with almost any materials you find around and also expend little money on the hydroponic cultivation of plants. They can also be designed to suit whatever open room you have (either inside or outside), and the different and creative ways to build them for that room are not constrained. Plants thrive very well in flood and drain systems, along with being affordable and straightforward to construct. The flood and drain method operates in theory much as it looks by inserting a nutrient solution into the plant root network - just periodically and not continuously. How a flood and drain hydroponic system functions very quickly. The central part of the flood and drainage network includes containers in which plants grow. It may be just one plant or several plants in sequence. A timer switches on the valve, and water (nutrient solution) is injected into the main part of the device by tubing from the reservoir using a submersible well/water pump. The nutrient solution fills the network (influxes) until it exceeds the predefined overflow tube height such that the roots of the plants are soaking. The overflow tube would be roughly 2 cm below the top of the rising newspaper.

When the tank is full of water, it flows down through the river, where it is recirculated again into the network. The overflow tube determines the water volume in the flood and drainage network, which guarantees that the water (nutrient solution) will not spill the top of the device as long as the pump is running. When the engine is turned off, the water is pumped back to the river via the pipe.

3. N.F.T. (Nutrient Film Technique) System

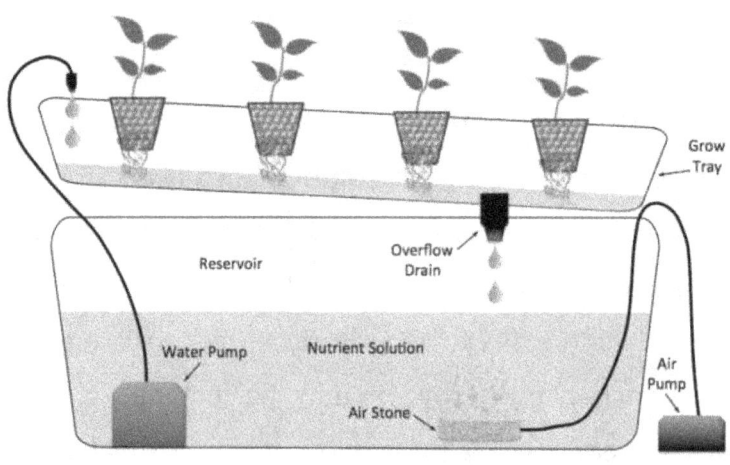

The N.F.T. (Nutrient Film Technique) method is also prevalent with domestic hydroponic farmers because of its straightforward design.

The N.F.T. schemes, though, are better suited to grow smaller plants such as different varieties of lettuce, which are more widely utilized.

In addition to increasing kale, several industrial farmers often develop various kinds of herbs and baby greens utilizing N.F.T. systems.

Although an N.F.T. method is built in a variety of different forms, they have the same function as a very shallow nutrient hydroponic solution.

Where the bare roots of the plants touch the water and may consume the nutrients, the biggest drawback to an N.F.T. device is that the plants are particularly vulnerable to water movement interruptions from power outages (or some reason).

Once the water starts flowing into the network, the plants can continue to wind very rapidly.

4. **Water Culture System**

Water systems are the easiest of the six hydroponic systems types. Technically, these systems are still very successful in hydroponic cultivation. Not only do home hydroponic farmers prefer to use water culture systems, but industrial producers also do utilize this form of the device on a broad scale.

The reason is that water cultivation systems are a clear and easy idea to develop. Moreover, the fact that the water system is also a cheap device to create is another explanation of why it is also popular with home growers.

While the principle is necessary, there are lots of creative ways of utilizing and constructing water culture systems from different materials.

5. Aeroponic System

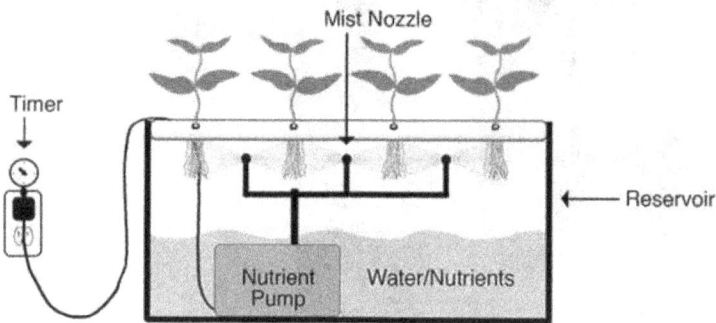

Although the aeroponic system is a fundamental term, it is, in reality, the most advanced of all six types of hydroponic systems. Nonetheless, constructing your own aeroponic system is very simple, and several home growers love to grow in them and even get outstanding results with this kind of hydroponic device.

As in every other form of hydroponic device, you may use a variety of different styles of materials and design configurations to suit your room - It can be applied even if your room and your creativity are tiny.
 Aeroponic structures usually use little or no rising media with certain advantages. The roots produce full oxygen, and as a result, the plants expand faster.

Yet, aeroponic systems do typically require less water than some other form of hydroponic device. Harvesting, particularly for root crops, is typically also easier.

However, there are still certain drawbacks of aeroponic devices in addition to being more costly to construct. The sprinkler heads will obstruct the creation of the dissolved mineral elements in the watertight of nutrients. Be sure you have extras to swap with when they clog while you clean them.

Moreover, since the plant roots remain in the center of the air through nature in aeroponic systems, the roots of plants are far more prone to dry up if the irrigation process is disrupted. Only a temporary power loss (for whatever reason) would, therefore, cause your plants to die far faster than any other form of hydroponic system. There is also a reduced margin of error with nutrient rates, particularly true high-pressure systems in aeroponic systems.

Chapter 13: Starting Seeds and Cuttings, Seeds Germination and Propagation of Clones

Remember where we have been coming from. I have also talked about the equipment used, the description of each system, how to set up your hydroponic system. Now, I will be discussing the method of propagation in hydroponics.

Starting Seeds and Germination

You are ready to start your hydroponic garden. After getting conversant with the equipment to use and how to set up your hydroponic garden. This is how to go about it.

Soak the seed to be planted for about 6-12 hrs. It is being soaked in a pot. I also said to use a growing media depending on your choice. The appropriate growing media is coco fiber. An important factor in preparing the seed for the growth stage is the size of the pot being used. It's advisable to use a small pot for a small number of seeds. That's because doing otherwise will make the seeds damp. A damp seed isn't the best to grow within hydroponics because it can cause root rot or even moldiness. Don't overlook this because it can cause underdevelopment of the seed.

Pour the seeds in a pot of volume 0.5L, sprinkle it with some water to be damp, allowing the water to circulate. After 5-10 minutes, add a few sprinkles if it's not damp enough. Some people make use of soil to start but we don't want our seeds to get soil dirty, right? Having to disengage the root from the soil carefully is also delicate. So, let us just stick to making the environment moist since that can perform the magic.

You need a propagator and light source to keep the environment moist and enable growth.

Some seeds grow very fast while some don't. The maximum period of germination s is between 3-5 days. So don't be bothered about late sprouting as the seed will surely germinate even though it takes time. Keep the environment moist because it aids quick germination

You might care to ask. How humid should the environment be? At what temperature should I grow the seeds? Those are very good questions as they determine the interim of seed germination. The starting temperature for the seeds should be about 20-25°C (68-77°F) and humidity should be about 60-70%. It can be reduced to 40% as the plant grows.

Another important piece of equipment in starting seed is the plug. I almost forgot to mention! The seeds are dropped into the plug to make clipping off easy after seed sprouting. How do you apply it? It's soaked with the seeds. You drop the seeds into it. I keep using the word" soak". Pardon my choice of words. Like I stated earlier, you aren't to soak in 100L of water rather you are to make the seeds damp. So when I use the word soak, you know what I mean by that.

I also didn't state that the water should be 20°C(room temperature).

To aid fast growth, apply a little bit of Formulex which is a seedling stimulant.

Let me summarize the whole process,

- Pour the seeds into a 0.5L volume growing pot(used for nursery plants)
- Dampen it with sprinkles of water.
- Make sure the seeds are in the plug as that's important for easy clipping after germination.
- Introduce a propagator which is used to maintain a moist environment and light source.
- Maintain a temperature of 20-25°C and humidity of 68-77°C.
- Add a little bit of seedling stimulant like Formulex.

Paper Towel Method

This method can be substituted in place for the first. Do you know why this method is advantageous?. You can witness the process of seed germination. And for those who get eager to see your seeds sprout, I will recommend this method for you.

In as much as this method has an upper hand over the other. Maximum Care has to be taken in carrying it out. This is because a paper towel is used just as the name implies. What's it used for? It is wrapped around the seed. Don't forget that a paper towel gets damp easily and may mess up the roots when it's due for transplanting. Hence, I advise you to use a thick paper towel. Maintain a temperature of 20°C. You can achieve this by putting it in a lockable Plastic bag. This makes it visible. You will be able to notice all changes taking place. After growth, it can be transferred into a growing medium.

You can then keep it in a light-void environment.

Cuttings

Cuttings are also called CLONES. It is used as an alternative to starting with seeds. If you are looking for a way to replicate the mother plant, then consider using the cutting method. Though, cloning works for some plants not all. You might think it's a bit difficult and you will prefer to resolve the seed method of propagation. Take a chill pill! And see how it can be done easily.

First of all, I'll enlighten you on this method. Why choose the cloning method anyways? You will get a replica of a plant faster using this method. The seed method takes more time compared to the cloning. This is why. In the cloning method, you make use of a growing plant to cultivate. Can you see that it's going to grow faster than a seed which you are yet to see signs of sprouting?

Another reason is that in a situation where you don't have seeds to grow, you can take cuttings from a plant and grow. It's less stressful than getting seeds. Cloning can also produce special characteristics or modifications that you can't get in a starting seed method.

- What are the procedures?.
- To extract cuttings from a plant, you need the following materials;
- A razor blade (a sharp one preferably, that means it must be new).
- Support (wood or plastic preferably)
- A plastic container
- A growing medium(Rockwool, coconut fiber)
- A seed tray
- Spray bottle
- A rooting stimulator like Formulex
- Alcohol.

So, you ask how do I utilize these materials?. You'll see that in a few.

When you want to take cuttings, make sure you select a healthy plant.

The growing medium to be used should be soaked. After which it should be punctured to fit the cutting in. Lest I forget, whatever material you will be using, make sure it is sterilized. The Alcohol should be poured on the blade and the cutting blocks hot glass to be used. After which it will be filled with rooting stimulator.

- How do you take the cuttings?
- This step is very delicate and must be handled with care.
- Take the cutting from the internode and some leaves with a sharp razor blade.
- Drop it into a shot glass containing the rooting hormone(a fluid)
- After which it should be dipped into the rooting medium to be used (Coco fiber for example).
- You must note that the cutting is open to certain diseases and microorganisms like bacteria, fungi. Hence, it must be taken care of properly.

The cutting dipped in the rooting medium should be sprayed with water to make sure it grows.

Chapter 14: Problem and Troubleshooting

Green Growth

Each hydroponic cultivating framework utilizes water and plant supplements. Lamentably, any place you have water, supplements, and light you will inevitably have green growth development. This is a major issue since green growth pulls in organism gnats, and parasite gnats will harm the foundations of your plants. To forestall green growth, a hydroponic framework must restrain the presentation of the supplement answer for the light at every possible opportunity. The supplement repository ought to be produced using a dim or misty material. The supplement store ought to have a top. Openings in the supply top ought to be no greater than the hydroponic siphon hose and the water bring the pipe back.

The plant holder should fit firmly into the opening, hindering any light from entering.

The framework itself ought to be moderately light confirmation. The shaky area in numerous frameworks is the place the plant openings have been produced in the framework. Plant gaps ought to be no greater than would normally be appropriate to hold the development medium (for example a got pot or rockwool solid shape). If the development medium is being watered from above, for example, with a trickle framework, a top ought to be utilized over the medium to limit the uncovered territory. Dribble producers can likewise be made to run underneath a light confirmation top, yet this will keep you from seeing trickle producers that have stopped up. Any plant openings not being utilized ought to be topped or secured with dim or dark material.

Hydroponic System Leaks

High weight frameworks are bound to spill than low weight frameworks. The most widely recognized hotspot for spills in a hydroponic framework are cut fittings and trickle/shower producers that sneak out of position. Less frequently, root development can cause spills in a continually streaming framework by making water back up and spill out when there isn't sufficient room in the cylinders.

During a force disappointment, I once saw all the supplement arrangement channel from a framework once more into the supplement repository which was around 10 gallons excessively little. I have additionally observed a high weight siphon that was not associated firmly enough out of anywhere pass over its fumes hose and douse down the room. Many break issues can be kept away from essentially by utilizing a hydroponic framework planned around a low weight siphon, for example, an NFT framework or a DWC framework. Further holes can be forestalled by utilizing a supplement repository sufficiently enormous to hold all the water in your framework, and by utilizing pipes sufficiently huge to deal with the frameworks water stream much after noteworthy root development.

Obstructs

Obstructs cause the most problems with dribble frameworks and shower frameworks (counting aeroponics). Trickle/shower frameworks utilize high constrain siphons to drive supplement arrangement through exceptionally modest openings. Supplement channels and pre-channels can decrease the event of obstructing however won't dispense with it. If you pick one of these frameworks, be set up to invest additional energy every day checking each splash spout/dribble head and supplanting any that have quit working.

Accommodation of Use

How simple is it to clean a hydroponic framework in the middle of employments, and how simple is it to do a supplement arrangement change while the framework is being used. A "simple to clean" framework offers simple access to each surface inside the framework, either by hand or with a brush. A framework can be a cerebral pain to clean if there is no top and the gaps are excessively little, or if there are tight corners or inaccessible twists.

A framework ought to be anything but difficult to purge of its supplement arrangement, and the procedure ought to upset the plants/plant roots as meager as would be prudent. A framework ought to hold almost no of its unique supplement arrangement when discharged. The entire supplement arrangement change should just take three or four minutes, accepting you have a repository of room temperature water prepared to supplant the old supplement arrangement (in addition to a couple of additional minutes to check and modify the new arrangement).

Fickle Nature of Some Systems

The primary worry here is how a lot of time you need to spend checking and keeping an eye on a specific framework. Each framework will require it's supplement arrangement checked and balanced at any rate once per day, however, a few frameworks should be checked substantially more regularly to forestall different problems. Dribble frameworks ought to be checked a few times every day to ensure the producers have not stopped up a couple of hours without supplement arrangement could kill a plant (particularly in a quick depleting medium).

The equivalent is valid for shower frameworks, particularly aeroponics. If you are utilizing no developing medium by any stretch of the imagination, at that point your supplement arrangement depletes promptly immediately and inexplicably. No medium methods no support zone ensuring the foundations of your plants. On the off chance that a shower spout obstructs in an aeroponic framework, your plants could bite the dust in under 60 minutes. I propose checking aeroponic frameworks four times each day or more, not exclusively to check for stopped up splash heads yet, also, to check for broken siphons and force disappointments (which would be similarly harming).

The most solid/least fickle hydroponic frameworks are DWC frameworks and NFT frameworks. These frameworks are low support and should be checked just once per day.

Cost of Cleaning/Reusing a System

One of the primary cost with reusing a hydroponic framework comes when you need to supplant the entirety of the developing medium. If you are utilizing rockwool, for instance, you need to toss out the entirety of the old rockwool and supplant it with new rockwool for each new yield. This can without much of a stretch be a $100.00 cost (or progressively), even in a little framework. Different frameworks utilize got pots loaded up with extended dirt pellets, igneous rock, or another reusable develop medium.

Another arrangement is to utilize a DWC framework or NFT framework, which utilize next to no develop medium and for the most part develop the plant establishes in standing supplement arrangement (with air bubblers). These decisions not just spare you the cerebral pain of discarding the old develop medium... after some time, they likewise spare you a lot of cash.

Chapter 15: Best Plants for Hydroponics

Plants suitable for Hydroculture

First of all, it is necessary to know that cuttings rooted in water are ideal for starting hydroculture because, for them, it is much easier to adapt to the expanded clay substrate since it is mainly composed of water.

If you want to start with the gardening of hydroculture plants, there is a great variety to choose from. If you are a lover of aromatic herbs, the rosemary plant is perfect for growing in hydroculture if you start from cutting; otherwise, you can choose other types of ornamental and very decorative plants, such as Ficus, Calathea, Pothos, Dracena, and Philodendron.

All plants characterized by leaves of tropical origin are well suited to hydroculture, such as the orchid and all those species that present a rapid development to the root system.

And what about flowering plants? In these cases, the most recommended species for home hydroculture are Hibiscus, Spathiphyllum, Kalanchoe, Anthurium, or Saintpaulia. Still, nothing prevents you from trying to cultivate other types of plants as well.

What about succulents? Succulents have a more complicated situation since they do not tolerate excess humidity. Therefore the recommended species for hydroculture are aloe, succulent

plants, and - as anticipated above - orchids.

Lettuce

Growing salad in hydroponics is elementary, much more than it might seem, even for those who start from scratch and approach the hydroponics world for the first time.

Once you have identified the variety of salad that best suits your needs and tastes, you must obtain the seeds that you will easily find online. Then you will have to buy rock wool cubes (Rockwool) and clear jars, a mini-green to store them in the warm, in a protected environment and with net pots, designed precisely for the needs of plants that are grown with hydroponic and aeroponic systems. Therefore, a small hydroponic or aeroponic system will be needed.

The salad seeds must be placed inside the moistened rock wool cubes (it is recommended not to insert more than five seeds for each cube) only with water and then placed inside the mini-greenhouse, at a temperature that can oscillate between 73°F (23°C) and 82°F (28°C).

One aspect to check - when using rock wool cubes - is the amount of water they absorb, because an excessive amount of liquid could cause the roots to rot and drown them. For this, it is always advisable to check the liquid levels present and possibly wring out the cubes to let out the excess water.

With the right amount of water and the ideal temperature, lettuce seeds will begin to germinate after about 48 hours. When you see the first roots appearing from the rock wool cubes (both from the sides and the base), it means that the time has come to transfer the newly born seedlings to the unique mesh pots, which will first be filled with expanded clay and then settled in the hydroponic system you have chosen (or aeroponic). The seedlings inserted in the aeroponic system will then be fed with a unique nutrient solution based on water and fertilizers to provide everything they need. It is vital to avoid any fertilizer during the germination phase and then start with a halved dose compared to what is recommended on the package.

Fertilizers for the gardening of Hydroponic salad

By using suitable fertilizers and in the right dose, the roots of the lettuce seedlings are allowed to develop better and faster than they would use with a traditional gardening system, also because - in this way - the roots can receive and assimilate nutrients faster.

To grow the seedlings in a healthy and fast way, thus strengthening their root system to make it more robust, it is possible to opt for some special fertilizers, which contain fundamental substances capable of promoting and increasing growth, accelerating absorption nutrients, and keep the most common salad diseases away. Fertilizers play a central role in the life and health of the plant. Since the hydroponic and aeroponic system does not provide for the presence of fertile soil, to ensure that the salad receives all the nutrients, it is essential to use the right fertilizers to be able to grow plants properly. Strengthening the root system of salad plants and preventing pests means growing healthy, reliable, and vigorous plants capable of returning a good harvest.

Hydroponic salad: parameters to monitor

At this point, once the gardening has started, it is appropriate to keep under control some fundamental values for the health and growth of each plant, such as the pH, which will determine the ability - by the cultivated plant - to absorb the available nutrients correctly.

 For salad plants to absorb all nutrients correctly, the pH must be slightly acidic, and to ensure that it is always such, it is advisable to often monitor the situation with manual tests. For example, cheap and easy-to-use paper strips for pH testing can be used.

Tips and tricks for a perfect Hydroponic salad

To create a suitable and protected environment, it is recommended to repair and check the salad plants inside a grow box to make them grow well, healthily and faster, without weighing on the cost of the bill.

Among the advantages of using the grow box, there is undoubtedly that of being able to control the temperature than a larger environment more efficiently and, therefore, less controlled, better manage ventilation, ensure the right lighting (thanks to the reflective mylar sheet present inside the grow box which allows the light to be effectively propagated).

But when will you get your first salad crop?

Much depends on the variety chosen and cultivated, but - in general - it is possible to say that the time required varies between 4 weeks and 80 days. By choosing different varieties and managing the aeroponic system, you can have a fresh, tasty, and healthy salad at any time of the year.

To help grow, salad plants should be adequately lit: the best solution is to use HID discharge lamps or LEDs, but a good compromise can also be found by using fluorescent lamps.

To better manage the lighting of the salad plants, it is advisable to activate the lights for 12 hours a day, thus ensuring 12 hours of darkness.

For beginners, it is advisable to purchase a simple lighting set consisting of 4 CFL lamps, sufficient for home gardening.

Strawberries

Cross and delight of many professional and amateur growers, the strawberry is a problematic fruit, especially if grown out of season and in unsuitable environments. All difficulties are overcome, especially for those who choose the above-ground gardening, better known as hydroponic gardening.

The more than tested technique, especially in strawberry gardening, offers more than exciting advantages:

- Production is standardized;
- There is a considerable saving of energy and water, which is used more rationally;

- Production is better in quality and quantity;
- The problem of diseases, molds, and pests that multiply on contact with the ground is entirely forgotten.

Those who choose the hydroponic technique also have the opportunity to produce strawberries in at least two different periods of the year: from October to December and throughout April and May.

If we also take into consideration that once planted, the plants begin to bear fruit after 45 days. It is well understood why this choice is shared by many growers and lovers of indoor gardening.

Anyone who chooses to switch to this type of technique must first thoroughly wash the roots of their seedlings and insert them in a small pot that contains expanded clay or alchemy of vermiculite and perlite.

It is also essential to have a container that can hold at least 10 liters of water (for each seedling), better if impermeable to the passage of light to avoid the formation of algae and mushrooms.

Among the most popular hydroponic gardening methods for strawberries, there is the one called NFT hydroponics: to make it simple with this system; it is possible to achieve a good circulation of all the nutrients that the roots need. Everything is automated thanks to the use of a timer that alternates between full and dry moments, essential for the roots to have the right oxygenation.

It is essential to have the right fertilizer, which in this case, is composed of nitrogen and potassium and water with the correct pH, which should always be adjusted between 5.5 and 5.6. To make the job easier, there are active acidity regulators on the market.

Finally, you must have the right lighting, and in this case, the lamps for indoor gardening will be a potent ally.

Once you start your strawberry gardening, domestic or industrial, it is good to keep in mind that the plant must be regularly pruned: it is wrong not to cut excess leaves, especially before flowering. These will unnecessarily weaken the plant and could favor the creation of mushrooms that are particularly harmful to the future growth of strawberries.

Also, despite the impatience shared by many growers, it is good that the fruit is harvested only when red and ripe, better still if in times of darkness.

Tomatoes

Quality and quantity with Hydroponic tomato gardening

Tomato is a genuinely functional vegetable in hydroponic culture. It reacts very well to the so-called "soilless gardening," this because it can easily adapt to different types of substrate and does not require demanding agronomic management.

In tomato hydroponics, multiple substrates can be used:

- Rock wool
- Peat

- Perlite
- Coconut fiber
- Compost

And with all, you can achieve magnificent results. The only precaution that must be paid in the hydroponic gardening of tomatoes is the temperature. Indeed, excessive maxims could affect the floral drop and, therefore, on the quantity and quality of the product.

Kitchen herbs

The new home dream is to have a thousand and one aromatic herbs on the terrace or the balcony to flavor your dishes with a personal, fresh, and eco-friendly touch. This is why hydroponics has been so successful.

The Greeks already knew it, Francis Bacon spoke about it in 1627 and today hydroponics (literally the art of growing plants in water) is well appreciated in the industrial and domestic field.

The hydroponic gardening of aromatic herbs has five remarkable qualities:

- The yield of the product that is developed through indoor gardening is better;
- Growth is faster;
- The taste is more intense;
- The gardening technique is environmentally sustainable;
- Water expenditure decreases drastically.

With hydroponic gardening at home, it is possible to grow any aromatic plant, whether it is parsley, basil, thyme, rosemary, oregano. Still, you can also choose to grow lettuces, tomatoes, strawberries, and who knows what else.

In short, hydroponics allows at reduced costs and with a disarming simplicity to make your terrace or balcony a garden of wonders, a vertical garden, an urban oasis.

The roots of our aromatic seedlings will seek support on an inert substrate often made up of expanded clay, pralines, coconut fiber, or other similar materials. Of course, the irrigation that the plant receives must be rich in inorganic compounds that will be able to give it all the nutrients that generally come from the earth. Your gardening of aromatic herbs will surely provide unparalleled satisfaction.

Chapter 16: Frequently Asked Questions

I cultivate my garden, and my garden cultivates me. ~Robert Brault

I have tried to give you a basic, but thorough beginner's guide to the most common and popular gardening methods. The emphasis has been on the mechanics of gardening. Now I want to bring it all together by answering the questions people tend to ask once they decide to try their hand at gardening. Some of the answers may be repetitions of things you have already read, but that is okay. If it is important enough to put in here twice, it's important enough to read it twice. So, without further ado...

Q: Is it better to start from seed or seedling plants?

A: Most of the time you will do better if you start your flowers with seedling plants. The main reason for this is that flowers take much longer to mature than vegetables. The exception to this is zinnias and sunflowers. You will also find that planting iris and lilies using just the chromes will work just fine, too.

When it comes to vegetables, however, it is almost always better to start from seed, except for tomatoes, which need to be started indoors if you want to enjoy the fruits of your labor before the growing season is over.

Q: Is there anything to the old sayings about planting according to the signs of the moon and other such things?

A: Yes, most definitely! For example, a new moon pulls water up from the ground, which in turn, swells a seed and causes it to burst open (germinate). That is why planting within a day or two of the new moon causes quick productivity.

Q: What's the difference between garden soil and potting soil?

A: Potting soil is less dense. It contains little or no actual dirt/soil but is a combination of peat moss, vermiculite or perlite, sand, and even finely ground tree bark. Potting soil has also undergone a sterilization process to kill any weeds and seeds that would interfere with plant growth. Garden soil contains actual soil, so it is much denser and doesn't drain as well as potting soil, and it tends to get packed down in pots.

Q: What about succulents? Are they easy to grow?

A: Yes. Succulents, which include cactus, are very easy to grow. They require next to no care and prefer not to be watered very often. In fact, I know people who have beautiful cacti that grow well with only a tiny bit of water every month or so. There are so many varieties of succulents to choose from, you can have a diverse and attractive display with very little work on your part. NOTE: Succulents do best in containers in most parts of the country.

Q: Are berries easy to grow, and can they be grown in small areas?

A: Strawberries are very easy to grow and can be grown in an area as small as 5x5 feet. Strawberry plants are a lot like bunnies—they multiply rapidly. You will need to thin your plants out each spring before they begin to bloom. You do this by simply pulling some of the plants out of the ground. You will also have to break their runners to separate them from their 'parent' plant. Sell or give your excess plants to someone. Blackberries, blueberries, raspberries, and all other berries require a lot more room and attention.

Q: Is one kind of mulch better than another?

A: Mulch is a matter of opinion. When you think of mulch, you tend to think in terms of cypress, cedar, or pine wood chunks. But there are actually several other materials you can use for mulch. They include rubber, pea gravel, creek gravel, nut hulls, cocoa bean hulls, and lava rock. Deciding what you use to mulch your gardens (if you use anything at all) depends on many things. For example, if your garden consists primarily of perennials, or if you have an area of your yard designated for pots, rock is often your best option. It doesn't have to be replaced, it doesn't attract insects (like wood does), and it requires next to no maintenance. Vegetable gardens or flower beds you will be tilling or spading every season don't need mulch. And finally, be sure your pets won't ingest the nut hulls, cocoa bean hulls, or rubber, as all are toxic to them.

Q: What are community gardens?

A: Community gardens are gardens used and tended to by several individuals. Most community gardens rent space to people to use for growing vegetables and herbs. Each person is responsible for keeping their own area of the garden weeded, watered, and tended to. I'll be honest—I don't know how community gardens keep people from taking things that aren't theirs. I assume it's based on an honor system, which should work. If you participate in a community garden venture, you still need to have your own tools, fertilizer, pest prevention, and so forth. Community gardens can be a great way to enjoy raising your own herbs and vegetables as long as you don't get tired of traveling back and forth to take care of your space.

Q: How do I know what planting zone I'm in?

A: This map shows the different planting zones in the United States.

Q: What flowers attract hummingbirds and butterflies?

A: Impatiens, petunias, hollyhocks, honeysuckle, bee balm, columbine, lilies, and phlox are a few of the most popular hummingbird attractants. Hibiscus, coneflowers, butterfly bush, sunflowers, lilac, zinnias, sweet William, petunias, and dianthus are just a few of the many flowers that will bring butterflies to your garden.

Q: Is it better to overwater or underwater your plants?

A: Neither. You need to make sure your plants get the amount of water they need AND that their home (ground, raised bed, or container) has proper drainage. When your plant is getting too much water, leaves will become pale and yellow and the plant will look limp. If they aren't getting enough water, leaves will drop to conserve food and energy for the main part of the plant.

Q: I see all sorts of unconventional things being used as flower or vegetable containers. What special preparation, if any, needs to be done to use these things?

A: Using 'unconventional' items to pot plants and flowers in is a great way to add a bit of whimsy and personal flair to your landscape. Flowers and plants look fine in traditional pots, but they look spectacular in an old suitcase, a cowboy boot, a vintage child's dump truck or lunch box, a dresser no longer in good enough condition to hold clothes, or whatever else appeals to you. The only preparation you need to make is to ensure the container has adequate drainage, so plants don't become waterlogged.

FYI: Other unusual items you can use for your container garden include:

- Old tins

- Purses

- Wheelbarrow

- Baskets

- Old tires

- Wooden boxes

Q: What things are compostable?

A: The most compostable materials are:

- Vegetable peelings

- Leaves

- Straw

- Sawdust

- Pine needles

- Small sticks

- Bark

- Paper towel and toilet paper tubes

- Newsprint (not glossy)

- Dryer lint

- Eggshells

- Coffee grounds

- Dead plants

- Stale bread, crackers, cereal

- Burlap

- Livestock manure

Q: What things can't I compost?

A: You cannot compost:

- Diseased plants

- Meat, pasta, bones

- Synthetics

- Walnut hull, leaves, and twigs

- Pet manure

- Human waste

- Plastic

- Glossy paper

- Dairy products

Q: How do I know if my soil is too acidic?

A: You can have a professional soil test done without spending a lot of money. You can also do it yourself using nothing more than a sealable clear glass jar, soil from your garden, and water. To test your soil, fill the jar about half full of soil from the garden you want to test. Fill the jar the rest of the way with water, leaving about an inch of space at the top. Seal the jar and shake it vigorously. Let it set untouched for 24 hours. During this time the soil will separate into layers of silt, clay, and sand.

You also need to notice the color or tint of your soil. The lighter the soil's color, the less organic matter it contains. If this is the case with your soil, you need to add compost matter to it to help your plants grow.

Conclusion

Thank you for making it through to the end of the book, let's hope it was informative and able to provide you with all of the tools you need to achieve your goals whatever they may be.

Once you have all your garden measured out, sit down with your graph paper, let one square equal one square foot (adjust this if you have the graph paper with the tiny squares), and start putting this all down on paper. Have the top of the paper be north, and draw a little arrow pointing that way to look more official.

As you do, you will find that you'll need to keep running out to measure more things in the yard to make everything line up correctly. You've measured the house and driveway, for example, but wait, how many feet do you have between the driveway and the east corner of the house? So you measure that. Where exactly does the oak tree sit in relation to the fence and the house? So you measure that. The fence and the house are not lining up correctly. So you re-measure that and try to figure out if you transposed a measurement. The oak tree seems to have inadvertently shrunk, though you'd measured it twice. Maybe it's time to take up drinking. Well, okay, but only in moderation.

Of course, that's the way the old timers did it. (Note: I am not old.) These days, you can fix up a nice landscape plan on your phone using an app, or get a more elaborate program for your laptop that will do more than just move a tree symbol around until it looks like it's placed right.

Then it's time for the big step: drawing a plan. Measure your garden. To keep your plan simple, let one-half inch equal one foot. Outline the garden on your paper.

Protip: Once you have this step finished to your satisfaction, take this paper to the copier and make several copies, and use these as the rough drafts of your garden design.

Now play with that outline. Consider the height and width of these plants. Keep short plants in front and tall plants in back, and use those pictures you've clipped (whether out of a magazine or found on the internet) to make sure the colors match. Do you want soft colors, such as purple catmint, pink petunias, and silver Artemisia? Or do you want a fiesta of red salvia and "Yellow Boy" marigolds?

Also, consider when your perennials bloom. You may love purple asters and pink sea thrift, but that color pairing won't be happening, because the asters bloom in fall and the sea thrift blooms in spring.

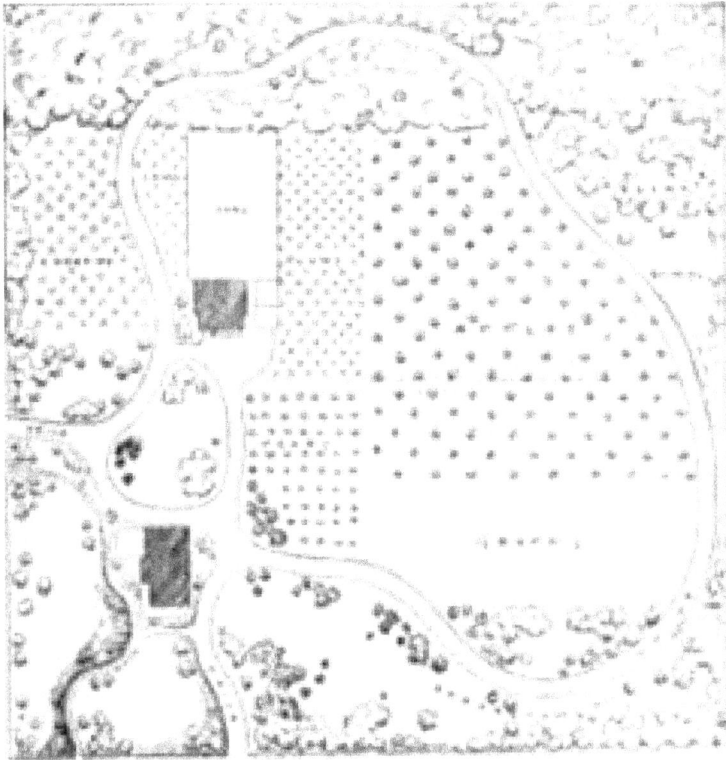

It's a good idea to put the tall plants in the back and short plants in front. Green side up. Match the plants to the amount of sun that's available. Set your shade plants near the trees, while the full sun plants will need to be right out in the sun.

As you draw your plan, generally a good rule of thumb is to arrange them by height – tallest plants in back, shortest ones in the back. Or, as with an island bed, tallest plants in the middle, going to the shortest on the edges. But you can also blend several different varieties of plants that are the same size, the same way as you would blend several different flowers in a flower arrangement, for a good blend of colors and shapes. And you don't have to be exact on regimenting sizes. A garden isn't a lineup of soldiers on dress parade, after all.

You can arrange the plants in any way. You can arrange them in a parterre, a formal setting with neat rows, tidy edged shrubs. Or you can have a wild, natural garden with plants arranged as if they were growing wild. Chances are you will be someplace between these two extremes in your own garden.

Also, to make more of an impact, plant your perennials in drifts of 3, 5, or 7. These groups provide more of an impact than just planting one of every plant (unless you have a specimen plant that's as big as an elephant).

Protip: It's a good idea to have a little out-of-the-way place in your garden where you keep extra plants – those you've picked up when on sale but can't find a place for, plants you've picked up out of curiosity, plants you've gotten from friends and neighbors that don't quite fit into your gardening plan, or things you need to find a proper place for but haven't gotten to yet.

This little garden can get helpful, though. If you have a plant in your regular garden that suddenly croaks, you can grab a full-grown specimen from your little side garden and pop it into your regular garden, if you're so inclined, thereby filling the gap.

You can also keep your cutting garden here, so you can just pop out the back door and cut a few flowers for bouquets inside the house. Then you won't have to swipe flowers from your front gardens and leave holes in it.

CPSIA information can be obtained
at www.ICGtesting.com
Printed in the USA
LVHW092208081220
673678LV00004B/38

9 781801 152242